Am I a
SAINT
Yet?

HEALING THE PAIN OF
PERFECTIONISM

M. SUE BERGIN

CFI

AN IMPRINT OF CEDAR FORT, INC.
SPRINGVILLE, UTAH

This is not an official publication of The Church of Jesus Christ of Latter-day Saints. The opinions and views expressed herein belong solely to the author and do not necessarily represent the opinions or views of Cedar Fort, Inc. Permission for the use of sources, graphics, and photos is also solely the responsibility of the author.

ISBN 13: 978-1-4621-1074-2

Published by CFI, an imprint of Cedar Fort, Inc., 2373 W. 700 S., Springville, UT 84663
Distributed by Cedar Fort, Inc., www.cedarfort.com

LIBRARY OF CONGRESS CATALOGING-IN-PUBLICATION DATA

Bergin, M. Sue, 1957- , author.
Am I a saint yet? : healing the pain of perfectionism / M. Sue Bergin.
    pages cm
Includes bibliographical references and index.
Summary: Offers relief to those who suffer from the debilitating condition of perfectionism.
ISBN 978-1-4621-1074-2 (alk. paper)
1. Perfectionism (Personality trait)--Religious aspects--Christianity. 2. Church of Jesus Christ of Latter-day Saints--Doctrines. 3. Perfection--Religious aspects--Church of Jesus Christ of Latter-day Saints. 4. Mormon Church--Doctrines. 5. Mormons--Conduct of life. I. Title.

BX8656.B53 2012
248.4'89332--dc23

                              2012035018

Cover design by Rebecca J. Greenwood
Cover design © 2012 by Lyle Mortimer
Edited and typeset by Whitney A. Lindsley

Printed in the United States of America

10 9 8 7 6 5 4 3 2 1

For my parents,

MARIAN SHAFER BERGIN
and ALLEN ERIC BERGIN

PRAISE FOR

Am I a SAINT *Yet?*

"I love this book! I love its practicality, wisdom, stories, humor, and approachable, hope-filled remedies. It will help us all to combat the kind of perfectionism that leads to self-conscious shame and despair instead of to Christ-conscious trust and peace."

> WENDY ULRICH, psychologist, author of *Forgiving Ourselves, Weakness Is Not Sin, The Temple Experience*, and the national bestseller *The Why of Work*

"Excellent! *Am I a Saint Yet?* is an inspiring, well written, practical guide that will help members stop berating themselves and start enjoying their journey as Latter-day Saints. We highly recommend this amazing, compelling book."

> GARY AND JOY LUNDBERG, authors of *I Don't Have to Make Everything All Better* and *Love that Lasts*

"Sue Bergin has written a treasure. The delight and peace that come from Sue's stories and analysis are profound. She considers positive and negative behaviors often found in the LDS culture, and offers insightful vision and wisdom in her exploration of a life well led as an active member of the Mormon faith. As an LDS woman I found myself in many of her chapters and enjoyed her thoughtful responses to territory that could have been troubling. This book is a must read."

> ELAINE E. ENGLEHARDT, PhD, distinguished professor of ethics, Utah Valley University

"*Am I a Saint Yet?* is a great resource for understanding and also changing perfectionism. Ms. Bergin's well-researched and thoughtfully written book can be of great benefit to anyone suffering from perfectionism, as well as those who work with them to overcome it. I highly recommend this book as a valuable addition to your library."

> BEVERLY SHAW, PhD, MFT, psychotherapist, Los Angeles, CA

When you climb up a ladder, you must begin at the bottom, and ascend step by step, until you arrive at the top; and so it is with the principles of the Gospel— you must begin with the first, and go on until you learn all the principles of exaltation. But it will be a great while after you have passed through the veil before you will have learned them. It is not all to be comprehended in this world; it will be a great work to learn our salvation and exaltation even beyond the grave.

— *Joseph Smith, Jr.*[1]

God wants to help us to eventually turn all of our weaknesses into strengths, but He knows that this is a long-term goal. He wants us to become perfect, and if we stay on the path of discipleship, one day we will. It's okay that you're not quite there yet. Keep working on it, but stop punishing yourself.

—*Elder Dieter F. Uchtdorf*[2]

As members of the Church, if we chart a course leading to eternal life; if we begin the processes of spiritual rebirth, and are going in the right direction; if we chart a course of sanctifying our souls, and degree by degree are going in that direction; . . . then it is absolutely guaranteed—there is no question whatever about it—we shall gain eternal life.

— *Elder Bruce R. McConkie*[3]

NOTES

1. Joseph Smith, Jr., in Joseph Fielding Smith, *Teachings of the Prophet Joseph Smith* (Salt Lake City: Deseret Book, 1977), 348.

2. Dieter F. Uchtdorf, "Forget Me Not," *Ensign*, November 2011, 120.

3. Bruce R. McConkie, "Jesus Christ and Him Crucified," in *1976 Devotional Speeches of the Year* (Provo, UT: Brigham Young University Press, 1977), 399–400.

ACKNOWLEDGMENTS

$\mathcal{I}$'m grateful first and foremost to my parents, Allen Eric Bergin and Marian Shafer Bergin, for encouraging me to write this book and for cheering me on consistently and lovingly along the way. We envisioned a collaborative, three-author effort until my father said, "I think this should be Sue's alone, from her experiences and her heart." I felt a bit abandoned at firs—but then grateful. I have grown immeasurably as I have studied, talked out ideas and issues with others, and put my experiences, thoughts, and healing to paper.

For thorough reading and suggestions that improved the manuscript (aside from my parents), I thank Wendy Ulrich, David Bergin, and Rust Tippett. My editor, Jennifer Fielding, was enthusiastic from day one and contributed astute comments throughout the writing and editing process.

My former psychotherapist, Clyde Sullivan, merits a paragraph all his own. His counsel that I be gentle with myself got through only after repeated attempts. With exquisite kindness and generosity of spirit, he persisted until I absorbed the message. He also introduced me to the phrase "muddling through" and encouraged me to use it often. At ninety (and legally blind for more than twenty years), he is perhaps the most non-perfectionistic—and joyful—Latter-day Saint I know.

Friends who listened, commented, and gave me insights have been invaluable. I thank Tami Harris, Ronda Walker Weaver, Jean Marshall, Elaine Englehardt, Charlene Winters, Cecelia Fielding, Cindy Settle Sandberg, David Sandberg, John Hoffmire, Shelley Hammond Hoffmire, Jeff Turley, and Susie Quebbeman.

CONTENTS

CONTENTS

PREFACE

*T*his book can be helpful to any Latter-day Saint who has a desire to spiritually progress, but it will likely be less helpful to those with a diagnosed (or diagnosable) emotional disorder or mental illness. The ideas and suggestions for alleviating the pain of perfectionism are not a substitute for professional help, though they can be a supplement if you're in counseling and discuss them with your therapist.

These pages also are aimed at Latter-day Saints who are trying diligently to meet the high standards of the gospel but often feel anxious, depressed, and not good enough. The book will be less useful to Latter-day Saints who have unresolved serious sin, although they too can benefit from many of the principles explored here.

Research about how to effectively treat perfectionism is in its infancy. Not all the healing approaches suggested in this book are empirically tested. Some are drawn from a variety of sources, including my own experience. (Studies have shown the cognitive approaches in Strategy 1 are effective.)

I have not attempted to make this a comprehensive tome about Latter-day Saints and perfectionism. While many issues could have been explored, some of them are beyond my scope or are treated more thoroughly elsewhere, such as body image challenges, obsessive-compulsive disorders, and preventing perfectionism in children. I hope many other Latter-day Saints will write on this topic and include dimensions of perfectionism that I have not covered here.

INTRODUCTION

Becoming a Recovering Perfectionist

In my 1974 Provo High School seminary class, I distinctly remember my teacher asking for a raise of hands from anyone who thought their parents were perfect. No hands.

"What about your bishop?" he said.

No hands.

"Your grandmother?"

None.

"The Prophet?"

My hand shot up—followed by peals of laughter.

"You think President Kimball is perfect?" my teacher asked.

"Yes," I said, my voice shrinking.

"No one but the Savior is perfect. Why would you think President Kimball is perfect?"

Humiliated by my apparent defective gospel understanding, I sputtered out a response: "The scriptures say we're supposed to be perfect, so it must be possible. If President Kimball can't get there, how can anyone get there?"

I don't remember the ensuing discussion, just my feelings of confusion and embarrassment. As a budding perfectionist, this public display of my flaws created such deep feelings of shame that the memory is indelible. The irony of experiencing this shame around the very issue that was causing it—my misunderstanding of the Savior's commandment to "be ye therefore perfect"—resonates with a heartbreaking reverberation these many years later.

Thankfully I am no longer a budding perfectionist but rather a recovering one. I have experienced the public humiliation of performing inadequately in front of others and the private desperation of believing I can never be good enough. I also have experienced the sweet relief of discovering that the Savior's Atonement applies to me, that I can be "enough" with his grace, that I don't need to be better than the best or "truer than true," as Elder Bruce R. McConkie once described the overreaching of perfectionism.[1]

This book is the result of my journey along the counterfeit path of salvation-by-perfectionism and my return to the true path through the healing and refining power of the Savior's Atonement.

In these pages, we'll explore three strategies for managing perfectionism—mining the power of your thoughts, saying no to the comparison trap, and nurturing your spirituality. The strategies come first and foremost from gospel principles. I have integrated them with social science research, thoughts from my own life as a recovering perfectionist, experiences from my work as a hospice chaplain, and consultation with several clinical experts, including my parents, Marian S. Bergin and Allen E. Bergin. Marian was a licensed clinical social worker in private practice for twenty years. Allen was a professor of psychology at Columbia University and Brigham Young University for a combined forty years and also worked in private practice. Now retired, both have decades of experience treating hundreds of clients who suffered from perfectionism.

The idea for this book grew from our discussions about perfectionism over a period of years. I remember in particular my father recalling a discussion in his Brigham Young University psychology class about reports that Latter-day Saints experience a high rate of depression. He asked the eighty class members if they thought the LDS culture fosters depression. He was surprised when the overwhelming majority said "yes." An in-depth discussion followed about why. They reached a consensus that some of the depression results from feeling pressure to be perfect, or more accurately, feeling pressure *to appear to others* as though they're perfect. The BYU class was not a scientific study, of course, and the causes for a problem such as depression will always be numerous and complex.[2] But the class's basic assessment rang true to the three of us.

We also explored together how perfectionism is not unique to Mormon culture but is an epidemic in North American culture—and increasingly in world culture. From Los Angeles to Beijing and everywhere in between, all of us get endless perfectionistic messages from advertisements, television shows, movies, books, radio—you name it. Everywhere are images of perfect bodies, perfect hair, perfect teeth, perfect cars, perfect homes, perfect romantic relationships, and perfect children. If we absorb the messages, we can feel pressure to be perfect in all these ways.

Over time, it appears that the LDS culture in North America has developed its own version of these expectations. Many Latter-day Saints put pressure on themselves and on each other to have in perfect order not only their houses and bodies and jobs but also their spiritual life—or at least the outward signs of it. Our scriptures must look well-worn and well-marked, our husbands should be progressing on the church leadership ladder, our wives should be sweet (but not too sweet!), and we must say our missions were the best years of our lives, even if they weren't. Studying the scriptures and having a sweet disposition and deeply valuing our mission experience are good things, of course. Where we get in trouble—and fall into depression and discouragement—is when we're motivated by fear and appearances rather than by a heartfelt desire to be more like Christ.

It's important to make a careful distinction here between the gospel of Jesus Christ and the culture that grows around any organization of imperfect people. The gospel is as perfect as its author, and it is divine. If everyone in the Church lived it perfectly, no one would have any problems, and we would all by happy and emotionally healthy all the time. But, of course, we are not perfect. We make mistakes, big and small, serious and not-so-serious, with brief effects and long-lasting effects. We sin to large and small degrees, sometimes with fleeting consequences and other times with lifelong consequences. And we are often oblivious to the hurtful impact of our behavior on others, leading us to continue and repeat our injuring attitudes and actions.

So no one set out to create a culture that nevertheless can sometimes be fertile ground for perfectionism. In fact, in recent years our leaders have repeatedly cautioned us against this problem, and I refer to their counsel throughout these pages. The fertile ground, especially in local wards and stakes, continues in many ways. It means that someone with perfectionistic tendencies, like me, is more likely to absorb imperfect religious instruction in ways that can harm his or her spirit. We all hear through the filter of our own experiences, temperaments, and biases, then attach meanings to messages that confirm what we already believe about our world.

For example, a woman with perfectionistic filters found herself feeling depressed by a sister's story at a stake women's conference several years ago. The speaker spoke about keeping romance alive in marriage, and the woman who was present remembers:

> She related how she and her husband have a tradition on their anniversary. Every year for more than twenty years, she said, she gets out her wedding dress and puts it on. She did not say, of course, "See how thin I am, even after more than twenty years of marriage." And I'm sure she did not intend to put down the women listening to her. But very few of them would be able to fit into their wedding dresses, and I could see the deflated emotions on their faces. The message that they did not measure up to this unrealistic standard—however unintended—was there.

Someone without perfectionistic tendencies might feel momentarily disheartened by the above situation but would brush it off, go home, and not give it another thought. A perfectionist, however, would likely ruminate on this account, compare herself, find herself wanting, and spiral into a funk. She might get out her own wedding dress and shed tears over her current weight. She likely would then be irritable with her husband and children, though they wouldn't have a clue why. Her husband might get another dose of her discouragement that evening when she turned down his romantic overtures because she felt fat and unattractive.

Pressure to appear perfect can also be found in the tension we feel when someone's experience seems at odds with a gospel principle. As with all cultures, the LDS subculture sometimes creates myths around sound principles, such as the principle of prayer. While the Lord has told us he will answer our sincere prayers, an unrealistic cultural misunderstanding has developed among some that a person who doesn't get a clear answer to a prayer must be insincere, unworthy, or asking for the wrong thing. If the formula doesn't work exactly as we perceive it, we blame the person trying to use it. When Latter-day Saints see this blaming, they learn not to risk discussing a difficulty of their own that might result in blame aimed at them. They go underground with their perceived imperfections, leaving only the "perfect" appearance on the surface.

I witnessed this kind of pressure in a Relief Society meeting several years ago. The teacher was talking about not relying on others for our testimonies. Comments were made about the importance of "having oil in our lamps" and that if we don't, we could be locked out from the Lord, like the five virgins in the New Testament parable (Matthew 25). A sister raised her hand and related, weeping as she talked, how she had prayed diligently over a long period of time for a more sure witness that the Church is true but had not received one. As she finished, the tension in the room was palpable. People didn't know what to say. A few women tried to assure her that she would eventually get her witness if she remained faithful, but their efforts were awkward. It was clear that it made us uncomfortable to have to deal with this sister's experience. The silence and clunky reassurances did little to help her with her feelings of disappointment and inadequacy.

Group experiences like these can powerfully influence everyone present. The reactions will vary depending on a person's history and personal approach to her own confusing experiences. While some women in Relief Society that day might not have given the incident another thought, others likely thought about it a great deal. Some might have said to themselves, "I get my answers quickly. I wonder what's wrong with her?" Or "I've had the same problem but have always been afraid to say anything about it. Now I know I shouldn't!" Those with perfectionistic tendencies likely thought something like, "Wow, she really looked like a fool in front of everyone. I will *never* risk that."

Group pressure to fit the "perfect" mold stunts our spiritual growth whenever it results in setting aside our distressing experiences rather than examining them. It's difficult to learn from such experiences unless we feel safe to look at them, ponder them, and discuss them with trusted others. If we don't do these things, we lose important opportunities to deepen and mature our faith.

Deepening our faith in Jesus Christ is ultimately what this book is about. We are not perfect and we won't be perfect in mortal life, no matter how hard we try. We cannot earn eternal life by our own efforts, however "perfect" we try to make them, but only by His mercy and grace.

As we come unto Him, we can eventually be perfected *in Him* (Moroni 10:32, emphasis added).

This is not to say that the requirements for eternal life can be watered down. The Lord asks nothing less from us than transformation. For disciples committed to enduring to the end, the trials of body and spirit that produce this mighty change will be "knee-buckling" as Elder Jeffrey R. Holland recently put it.[2] What we *can* do is better recognize the limits of our humanness and more fully embrace the reality that we cannot become "new creatures" without Christ (Mosiah 27:26). We don't have to do the transforming alone. In fact, we *cannot*. We become his sons and daughters only through his redeeming power.

I hope that as you read these pages, you will better understand how perfectionism distracts and diverts you from your Savior's outstretched arms and will find ways you can gently guide yourself back to his embrace.

NOTES

1. Bruce R. McConkie, "The Probationary Test of Mortality," Salt Lake Institute of Religion devotional, January 10, 1982.

2. There is no evidence that depression is more common in Latter-day Saints than in other populations, though it is still common. For a detailed discussion of this topic, see the Foundation for Apologetic Research and Information (FAIR) website at www.fairlds.org and search for "statistical claims antidepressants."

ANSWERING THE
QUESTION

*B*efore proceeding further, I want to answer the question posed in the title of this book, "Am I a Saint Yet?"

The answer is likely a resounding "Yes!"

King Benjamin's words are quite clear about how we become saints—"through the Atonement of Christ the Lord, [becoming] as a child, submissive, meek, humble, patient, full of love, willing to submit to all things which the Lord seeth fit to inflict upon him, even as a child doth submit to his father" (Mosiah 3:19).

If you have been baptized, if you have received the Holy Ghost and strive to have the Spirit with you, if you understand what it means to put off the natural man or woman and are struggling toward that, if you're a good person who's working diligently at becoming better—*even though you fall far short*—then you are a saint. (If you have a few things to do before meeting this definition, that's okay.) That doesn't mean you necessarily feel comfortable calling yourself a "saint." I don't either. But technically by this definition, you probably are.

The fact is, you're also a sinner. The challenge is in accepting that it's part of our Heavenly Father's plan that we be both saint and sinner during mortal life. As the years go by, we hope the saint elements begin to overtake the sinner elements, but we'll always be some of both as long as we're mortal.

So let's dispense with that question and get on with the healing.

CHAPTER 1

What Is Perfectionism and Why Does It Hurt?

I'm trying so hard to be good, but I'm always anxious. Why can't I feel the peace that other Latter-day Saints talk about?

I'm afraid if I let go of guilt that I'll stumble and fall. I have to keep the guilt going to become a better person.

I wonder constantly, if I were to die right now, would I be in the celestial kingdom? I know God's merciful, but he has to do what he has to do.

I feel humiliated if anyone knows I have a problem with anything.

*C*an you hear the pain in the voices of these Latter-day Saints? Do you identify with any of them? Maybe you too worry obsessively about your eternal salvation, thinking you can never measure up. Perhaps someone you love feels guilty almost all the time or obsessively tries to improve at every moment. Possibly you focus on outer evidence of your value, such as a flawless body, straight A's, a prominent church calling, or perfectly obedient children. Maybe you fear that if you dare to tell yourself you're on the right track, you'll become arrogant or prideful.

All four of these voices are from real people. One of them is mine from a time when I suffered from perfectionism—the relentless drive to be faultless that creates depression, anxiety, and discouragement. Perfectionism is the determination to never make a mistake so we can ward off others' criticism, the need to project a picture-perfect image to others in the hope we can calm our inner panic about our failings, the longing to be so especially righteous or beautiful or accomplished that others are compelled to love us—including God.

You might be surprised by this. Maybe you thought perfectionism means the admirable striving to become a better person, line upon line, until achieving perfection. Or that we all need some perfectionism to motivate us to keep moving upward. Or that the world would be a better place if more people were perfectionists. It seems logical that marriages would be better, families more harmonious, wards more unified, friendships more rich, and the workplace more rewarding if everyone were always striving to be perfect.

Perfectionism, as I'm using the word throughout this book, is not a healthy striving for righteousness or excellence. It is, in fact, the adversary's counterfeit path to improving ourselves. It beckons us toward a long detour away from the true path by deceiving us into believing we must earn salvation through our own efforts. It distracts us with unrealistic expectations and sidetracks us with an emphasis on external performance rather than internal goodness (an intimidating goal by itself, to be sure!). Perhaps most telling, perfectionism does not give us the peace and serenity we long for and that the true path of Christ offers. Instead, it spawns feelings of desperation, anxiety, and fear.

While working to become a better person is healthy and righteous, perfectionism works against our emotional health and sabotages our efforts to become more like Christ. If you are perfectionistic, you set your standards so high that they cannot be met. When you fail to live up to them, you're so disappointed in yourself that you become discouraged and depressed. You might begin to avoid situations where you could fail again, making it difficult to progress and improve in incremental, more manageable ways. You may hold the same unrealistic standards for others, who also can't live up to them. As others shrink from you, trying to avoid your criticism, you might become self-hateful, destroying your capacity for healthy and renewing relationships. Perhaps most heartbreakingly, you might also miss the chance to understand Christ's love for you just as you are—and the deeper joy such an understanding could give you.

From a clinical perspective, perfectionism can range from mild to severe. Many people have tendencies without having a full-blown version of the syndrome. (Perfectionism has not yet been identified as a disorder by the American Psychiatric Association but is being considered for the next edition of its *Diagnostic and Statistical Manual of Mental Disorders*.) According to researcher Sidney J. Blatt of Yale University, the consequences for those on the severe end of the spectrum can be dire: "Intense perfectionism and severe self-criticism are associated with a vulnerability to severe depression and a serious potential for suicide."[1]

With this clarified definition, you might at this moment be criticizing yourself. "I'm such a perfectionist—yet another thing that's wrong with me!"

It is indeed possible that you have some tendencies in that direction. Almost everyone is a perfectionist to one degree or another. If you're berating yourself, please gently replace the scolding with thoughts like, "Hmmmm—this is interesting. I'd like to learn more." Or "Ah-hah! There's a name for my pain. That's something I can work with."

An Unexpected Vulnerability

People of virtually all religious faiths are more susceptible to perfectionism because their consciences are especially educated to recognize sin and feel guilt. The line between appropriate guilt and inappropriate guilt can sometimes be thin and hard to define, and many people of faith jump to inappropriate guilt without careful thinking. (An obsessive-compulsive form of religious perfectionism has been named "scrupulosity disorder." Research about it is in its early stages.) In my research for this book, I came across many laments from those of other faiths who worry about their standing before God. This quote from Father Thomas M. Santa, a Roman Catholic priest, touched me in particular: "It has often been hard for me to believe I'm loved by God exactly as I am and that the love God has for me isn't dependent on some future moment of perfection. It's often been a struggle for me to embrace my human condition—to acknowledge my faults and my failings—while learning not to dwell on them or perceive them as something that separates me from God. Some days I have a sense of peace and well-being. Others I don't."[2]

Rabbi Harold S. Kushner, perhaps most famous for his book *When*

Bad Things Happen to Good People, also wrote *How Good Do We Have to Be?* In it, he describes encountering many people in his ministry and his counseling practice who don't feel good enough:

> Much of the unhappiness people feel burdened by, much of the guilt, much of the sense of having been cheated by life, stems from one of two related causes: either somewhere along the way, somebody—a parent, a teacher, a religious leader—gave them the message that they were not good enough, and they believed it. Or else they came to expect and need more from the people around them—their parents, children, husbands, or wives—than those people could realistically deliver. It is the notion that we were supposed to be perfect, and that we could expect others to be perfect because we needed them to be, that leaves us feeling constantly guilty and perpetually disappointed.[3]

So Latter-day Saints are not alone in our quest for perfection or in our fears about achieving it. But we experience that quest and those fears in some ways that are distinctive, and the spiritual and emotional risks are perhaps heightened if we have "zeal without knowledge," as Hugh Nibley said.[4] No other religion emphasizes quite like ours that the ultimate purpose of our existence is literally to become as perfect as God is. If we don't temper our zealous efforts toward that goal with knowledge—an accurate and clear understanding of the Atonement—we become vulnerable to the risks.

The Risk of Underestimating Mercy and Grace

While the plan of salvation is designed to bring us eventually to perfection, our emphasis on good works sometimes overshadows our bedrock doctrine that it is only through Christ's grace and only in a continuing process after this life that we can reach that state. When we behave righteously because we have a sincere desire to access the Savior's atoning power and become more like him, we are on the true path. When we behave righteously because we fear looking imperfect to others—or even to ourselves—we are on the counterfeit path. Our fear and anxiety can keep us awake at night, make us prickly toward loved ones, and cause us to work at pleasing others in ways that hurt us and them.

Church leaders regularly warn us against unrealistic expectations of perfection, especially the idea that we can, or are expected to, become perfect in this life. President Gordon B. Hinckley said:

We will not become perfect in a day or a month or a year. We will not accomplish it in a lifetime, but we can begin now, starting with our more obvious weaknesses and gradually converting them to strengths as we move forward with our lives.[5]

Notice his wording. We *begin* in this life. The process is *gradual*. Our purpose is to *move forward*, not to reach a defined place within a defined amount of time.

Elder Marvin J. Ashton urged Latter-day Saints to "come to terms" with the frustration we often feel when we experience the gap between our idealistic standards and our actual less-than-perfect behavior.

I feel that one of the great myths we would do well to dispel is that we've come to earth to perfect ourselves, and nothing short of that will do. If I understand the teachings of the prophets of this dispensation correctly, we will not become perfect in this life, though we can make significant strides toward that goal.[6]

Again, the standard is "significant strides." Not perfection.

And President Spencer W. Kimball said: "Perfection is a long, hard journey with many pitfalls. . . . It is not a one-time decision to be made, but a process to be pursued, slowly and laboriously through a lifetime."[7]

A *process*, not a product. Something to be *pursued*, not finished. Movement toward the goal *slowly*, not frantically or quickly.

The Risk of Post-Imperfect Syndrome

A second risk that accompanies such a lofty goal as eventual perfection is that when we fall short we might judge ourselves as having already failed—so why not fail so more? This "post-imperfect syndrome," as I call it, can be terribly damaging and painful.

Consider Bruce, a faithful member of the Church who has perfectionistic tendencies. Bruce recognizes he can't be perfect in all things but believes he can be perfect in some things, such as obeying the Word Wisdom. Part of this belief is that he must not consume any amount of caffeine in any form under any circumstance. One evening, he finds himself with a severe headache, and he takes a few aspirin he finds in the kitchen cupboard. He mentions this to his wife, and she tells him that particular brand includes caffeine. Bruce now has tarnished his perfect record. He then judges himself as incapable of success at being perfect even in this supposedly doable arena. So he gives up entirely on his goal and consumes energy drinks with great abandon. Since he can't meet the expectation he has set for himself (unrealistic as it was), he throws it all away.

Those without such perfectionist motives might not get this, but those with them can likely identify examples of this kind of episode in their lives. A more serious example has occurred in the lives of many "older" Latter-day Saint singles I know. As time goes by and marriage does not happen, many of us redouble our efforts to *make* it happen by trying to be especially righteous, especially obedient, and especially exacting of ourselves. Marriage and children are the highest blessings of life, and we believe that perhaps we haven't merited them yet. We shift from the young-adult belief that marriage happens naturally (as it does for most) to believing that we must "deserve" that blessing by being the best, most worthy person we can possibly be. (No matter that many of the married Latter-day Saints around us are not especially righteous or obedient. In our perfectionistic haze, we don't notice things that contradict our personal reality.)

If we make those redoubled efforts for a significant period of time and marriage still does not happen, we might judge ourselves to be undeserving, unblessed, and failures. If God has not blessed us with this ultimate blessing despite our righteous desire and our best efforts, we must be more dismally unworthy and undeserving than we thought. We might find ourselves feeling not only the loss of love from the spouse we have not found but also a loss of love from God himself. So why try? A period may follow of giving up on trying much at all to be righteous or obedient. The spiritual devastation can cut a wide and deep swath. For some the giving up becomes permanent.

Friends and family might judge men and women who go this route as having succumbed to prevailing worldly standards. While that could be a factor as well, at least some of the giving up is actually a perfectionistic judgment of self that success is impossible. The true cause of giving up is spiritual injury, some self-inflicted, but some inflicted by circumstances beyond one's control, some by well-meant but rickety application of gospel principles, and some by pharisaical cultural demands. Recognizing these factors does not constitute unrepentant refusal to take responsibility. It's acknowledging that as human beings we're all subject to pressures that, when unexamined, can take us off course. As we carefully unearth our own unexamined beliefs and motives and then sort out what the Lord asks of us and what our culture expects, we can liberate ourselves from these wild swings. Strategy 1 will help us with examining beliefs and motives in more detail.

The Risk of Superabundant Opportunities for Comparison

All human beings compare themselves to others to some degree, and all perfectionists do it more than most. LDS perfectionists, however, have especially abundant opportunities to measure themselves against others. With a Church organization made up almost entirely of volunteers, we have regular chances to witness super-competent people deliver great talks, teach fantastic lessons, confer inspired priesthood blessings, and pull off seamless ward parties. We also have more than ample opportunities to fail publicly as we give lousy talks, deliver under-prepared lessons, confer uninspired priesthood blessings, and plan ward activities that flop. Many of us tend to compare our flops with the super-competent Saints' successes, and we end up deflated in the process. Strategy 2 is all about handling this toxic tendency to compare.

How Did I Get This Way?

It's likely that some people are born with a tendency toward perfectionism. While no one has discovered a gene for this trait, researchers have found in general that most personality traits have at least partial roots in biology. This means hard-wiring tendencies might be present in some people, but environmental influences can bring out this potential.

One of the more common circumstances that can lead to perfectionism is important people in your early life who gave you attention mostly when you performed well. They may have expressed love mostly for external performance, such as getting good grades, excelling athletically, looking good, playing a musical instrument well, or keeping things neat and orderly. If they acted embarrassed or ashamed of you when you didn't perform to their expectations instead of encouraging you and reminding you of your strengths, you likely learned to draw your sense of self-worth at least partly from external approval. As an adult, rather than feeling inherently valuable as a child of God, you may feel your value shifting according to your successes and failures—and what you and other people think or say about them. To defend against these painful fluctuations, you try to be perfect. But, of course, perfection is not possible. When your performance falls short, as it inevitably does, you may become discouraged and depressed.

Parents who directly criticize can cultivate perfectionism as well. Many children bombarded with critical messages will work hard to prevent the painful criticism by behaving as perfectly possible. Those with a sensitive disposition will take criticism especially hard. If they're so good that there's nothing to criticize, the pain diminishes. So they get "gooder" and "gooder."

Parents who are perfectionistic themselves are more likely to pass on this characteristic to their children. Many don't realize they have a problem and are unaware that they might be negative models. In fact, some believe they're preparing their children for the hard realities of life by insisting they become high achievers and maintain exacting standards. High standards in and of themselves are not problematic. They are, in fact, necessary for individual growth and for building a better world. However, when parents communicate that their children must meet their standards *as a condition for receiving love or approval,* they cross the line into harming rather than helping their children. If they criticize rather than support and encourage as their children are learning and trying to build their skills, they create fertile ground for perfectionism.

Is Perfectionism a Women's Issue?

No public studies of perfectionism among the LDS subpopulation exist, which makes it impossible to scientifically answer the above question. From mere observation, most Latter-day Saints I talk to believe more LDS women are perfectionistic than LDS men. They often speak of the "superwoman" syndrome, which is widespread among the larger US population but appears to be magnified in the LDS subculture. General conference talks frequently speak of women's feelings of inadequacy and reassure them they're doing fine while men are frequently taken to task for shortcomings. This is compelling evidence that LDS women at least are perceived to be more perfectionistic than LDS men.

What's the Difference between Perfectionism and High Standards?

It's important to understand that holding high standards is not the same as being perfectionistic. We can find enormous satisfaction and be a blessing to the world if we do quality work in a profession, become superior at a skill, work to be more charitable toward others, and strive to be more in tune with the Spirit. If you're a school teacher dedicated to excellence, you can influence thousands of children for good. If you're a parent and work hard to do the best you can in that role, you are an agent for profound goodness as you raise happy and emotionally healthy—though imperfect—children. If you are a disciple of Christ, you are at peace with yourself and kind toward others.

Perfectionism, then, is not putting a high value on excellence. Rather, perfectionism sneaks up on us when we obsess over a task beyond the point that is useful, when we berate ourselves after a failure, when we believe nothing we do is good enough, when we impose our impossible standards on others, and when we forget to access the Lord's grace that we all need every day.

Take a look at the chart below, which distinguishes between harmful perfectionism and helpful beliefs about high standards.

PERFECTIONISM VS. HIGH STANDARDS[8]

Perfectionism	High Standards
1. You are motivated mostly by a sense of duty. When you don't do what you think you should, you feel guilt out of proportion to your behavior.	You are motivated by a deep sense of right and wrong. You feel guilt when you do something wrong but are able to let go when you've done what repair you can.
2. You feel driven to be better than everyone else, but even when you think you've succeeded, you don't feel satisfied or at peace.	Your strivings to be a better person give you feelings of satisfaction and peace, even if you fall short.
3. You believe you must earn other's love and acceptance by being "special" or righteous or intelligent or accomplished.	You possess a strong sense of your eternal value as a child of God. You do not believe you must earn others' love and friendship by impressing them.

4. The idea of failure terrifies you. When you don't achieve goals that matter to you, you sink emotionally, feeling like a total failure.	You're not afraid to fail. Although failure is disappointing, you realize some failure is inevitable, and you see it is an opportunity to learn.
5. You think you must always be strong and in control of your emotions. You fear that sharing vulnerable feelings like sadness, insecurity, or anger will cause others to think less of you.	You're not afraid to show your vulnerabilities. You find that sharing your feelings and being open about your weaknesses with people you trust helps you progress and feel closer to others.
6. You feel humiliated when your limitations and weaknesses are exposed.	You feel humble and willing to learn from your mistakes.

Adapted with permission from David D. Burns, The Feeling Good Handbook (New York: Morrow, 1989).

Again, I want to caution you. If you're reading the items in the left-hand column and seeing yourself in them, your first impulse might be to criticize yourself. I urge you to resist that impulse. Rather than telling yourself you'll never be good enough, try saying to yourself something like, "It's good to see that others are experiencing this too. With more information, maybe I can start healing."

Also remember that the items in the right-hand column are ideals. No one is this balanced and emotionally healthy all the time. Like all ideals, these are principles to aspire to, not yet another "should" that you can't measure up to.

As we try to follow our leaders' counsel, it is not always easy to perceive that we have angled off onto the counterfeit path. On the surface, perfectionistic behavior can appear healthy and productive. The key to the distinction is in two things: First, your motives, and second, how you feel about yourself and your life. Let's consider two real-life cases* to take a deeper look at what perfectionism looks like in real people's lives.

JESSICA

Jessica is an LDS mother who deeply loves her husband and three

---

* Jessica and Carlos are composites of several real-life people.

small children, faithfully fulfills her church callings, and serves others whenever she can. She works hard at a home business that has become successful. She spends hours at the gym each week to stay in shape.

From the outside, Jessica looks happy, successful, and beautiful. On the inside she feels constantly unhappy and on the edge of depression, if not in the depths of it. Why? Let's look beneath superficial appearances. Jessica works so hard at her job not because she has a wholesome drive for excellence but because she is preoccupied with wanting more money so she can have nicer clothes, newer cars, and a bigger house. And why does she want those? Because they create the image she wants to project to others—that she is happy, successful, and beautiful. Her many hours of exercise each week are motivated not by a desire to be reasonably healthy and attractive but by an obsessive need to be more attractive than anyone else. The deeper motive is fear. She is afraid of appearing unhappy, scared of being seen as unsuccessful, and terrified that anyone might think she's unattractive.

"Whenever I enter a room where there are other women, I quickly look around to make sure I'm the most attractive one there," Jessica says. "I usually am. When I'm not, I'm devastated. That makes me all the more determined to spend even more time at the gym, at the beauty salon, at the mall—whatever it takes to get back on top."

Jessica's preoccupation with work and her appearance is damaging her relationship with her husband and children. They feel sidelined and neglected. Her need to constantly compare herself with others makes it difficult for her to keep friends. She feels competitive even with her brothers and sisters.

"Here I am turning thirty-seven, and I'm still living in a starter home," she says. "My sister has just moved into a beautiful new home, and I can't bear to go see it. It just hurts too much."

Jessica's perfectionism is hurting her children, her husband, her siblings, and herself. Though this description of her makes her sound like someone you wouldn't like, she is in fact a lovely woman who longs to do the right thing and to feel at peace with herself. She doesn't understand her feelings, her motives, or her inability to move from an external, materialistic focus to a more internal, spiritual one.

CARLOS

Carlos is a twenty-something university student who has been married for five years. He's the oldest of seven children born to highly accomplished parents. His father was critical and taught his children that the consequences of decisions are permanent, so they must be made exactly right. Carlos finds himself asking many times a day things like: "Would Dad do this? What would Dad think about this? What would Dad think of me if he knew about this?"

Starting at about age fourteen, Carlos began to feel depression that he described in counseling as "oppression and darkness." He often criticized himself severely but made sure no one knew about any pain he was feeling. As an adult, he finds his life "tough," and he's always "tired of the struggle." He sees other people feeling happy and doesn't understand why he can't have those feelings, especially since he married a wonderful woman in the temple and has the blessings of a good mind, abundant talents, and access to a good education.

One of Carlos's greatest stressors is his inability to feel the Spirit despite his sincere efforts. "I try to have spiritual experiences, especially in the temple," he says, "but I don't."

Carlos, like Jessica, suffers from perfectionism. His chief motivation is fear—fear that he won't look good to others, fear that his father won't approve of him, fear that he will make a mistake. When he achieves things, which he does often, he feels little satisfaction.

Outwardly, both Jessica and Carlos may appear accomplished and enviable to others. Inwardly, each is suffering from anxiety, exhaustion, self-criticism, and depression. In chapter 3, we'll learn more about both Jessica and Carlos and their gospel-centered healing from perfectionism.

PERFECTIONISM AND SHAME

The underbelly of perfectionism is shame, that awful feeling when we do something we think is bad that we *are* bad—to the core. Shame researcher Brené Brown defines shame as "the intensely painful feeling or experience of believing that we are flawed and therefore unworthy of love and belonging."[8] She distinguishes between guilt and shame, explaining that shame equals "I am bad," while guilt equals "I did something bad." As a research professor at the University of Houston Graduate College of Social Work, Brown has studied shame for more than a decade. She says: "Recognizing we've *made a mistake* is far different than believing we *are a mistake.*"[9] For a more in-depth exploration of shame, see her book *I Thought It Was Just Me (but it isn't): Telling the Truth about Perfectionism, Inadequacy, and Power* (2007).

So I'm a Perfectionist. Now What Do I Do?

Most of us have at least some perfectionistic tendencies. That doesn't make anyone, including you, a terrible person but rather a human being with flaws, just like the other imperfect human beings around you. If your perfectionism is interfering with your life, you don't have to keep suffering. You can heal from this painful condition. As you follow the suggestions in the rest of these pages, you will find relief, peace, and an increased capacity for joy.

Notes

1.   Sidney J. Blatt, "The Destructiveness of Perfectionism," *American Psychologist* (December 1995): 1010.

2.   Thomas M. Santa, "Strength in Weakness," *Scrupulous Anonymous* (June 2009). Retrieved July 3, 2012 from http://mission.liguori.org/newsletters/pdf_archive/SA_0609.pdf.

3.   Harold S. Kushner, *How Good Do We Have to Be? A New Understanding of Guilt and Forgiveness* (Boston: Little, Brown and Company, 1996), 8.

4.   Hugh Nibley, "Zeal Without Knowledge," in *Approaching Zion* (Salt Lake City: Deseret Book, 1989), 63-84.

5.   Gordon B. Hinckley, "The Quest for Excellence," *Ensign*, September 1999.

6.   Marvin J. Ashton, "On Being Worthy," *Ensign*, April 1989.

7.   Spencer W. Kimball, "The Abundant Life," *Ensign*, October 1985.

8.   Brené Brown, *I Thought It Was Just Me (but it isn't): Telling the Truth About Perfectionism, Inadequacy, and Power* (New York: Penguin/Gotham Books, 2007), 5.

9.   Ibid., 13–14.

BREATHER

Consider Taking "Perfection" off the Table

When I was close to finishing the first draft of this book, I became increasingly uneasy with the approach of simply playing down perfection and playing up progress. As I pondered how to communicate some of the lessons I've learned about my own perfectionism, I realized that a good deal of the tremendous relief I have experienced has come as I've taken ideas about perfection entirely off the table. For me, this step—though I did not do it intentionally at first—has been a powerful strategy for reducing my anxieties and perfectionistic behaviors. As long as an expectation of "perfection" was still in the background, I couldn't find peace.

But the doctrine of eventual perfection is still there. One of the purposes of the Church remains "the perfecting of the Saints." Can I in good conscience recommend to others to take "perfection" off the table too? The answer is yes. For several reasons.

- The ultimate goal of perfection is something that cannot be achieved in this life. The teachings of our prophets are clear that perfection is a process that will continue into our post-mortal life. Because perfectionists are at special risk of spiritual injury,

23

it's an idea worth considering to simply focus on progress and set aside thoughts of perfection.

- The "perfecting of the Saints" purpose of the Church doesn't say "the perfec*tion* of the Saints." It says perfect*ing*. The "-ing" is critical. We're here on earth to begin a process but not to finish it.

- There's a vast difference between the application of Christ's grace in our mortal lives and the final application of His grace in the next life. His grace here on earth is to nurture and foster us as we progress along the mortal path. If we have regularly repented and endured to the end of our mortal lives, His grace in the next life (after a post-mortal process that we know little about), will "finish" our faith so that we then are perfected *in* Him and ultimately exalted to eternal life with Him.

You can't become perfect in this life. Not even close. For anyone with perfectionistic tendencies, it's emotionally unhealthy to think you can. What you *can* do is grow, develop, and become a better person a little at a time—with the Savior's help.

STRATEGY ONE

Mine the Power of Your Thoughts

Words, thoughts, and images are powerful. As a recovering perfectionist, you can choose to use that power to step away from hurting your spirit and instead nurture it.

In this section, you'll learn:

- Concrete ways to replace your damaging thoughts with healing ones.

- How an LDS woman and an LDS man used the power of their thoughts to begin healing perfectionism.

- How to adjust deeply ingrained sayings so that they help you rather than hurt you.

CHAPTER 2

Trading In Your Self-Injuring Self-Talk

As a man thinketh in his heart, so is he. (Proverbs 23:7)

The old adage that "sticks and stones can break my bones but words can never hurt me" is false. Words can indeed hurt. They can wound so deeply, in fact, that healing from them can be more difficult than healing from physical injuries. *Words matter.*

For perfectionists, *the words we say to ourselves*—our thoughts—are at least as important as words that others say to us. Often we don't wait for others to say things that hurt us. We beat them to it. To illustrate, try the following brief exercise.

- Slowly read the scripture that introduced this chapter: *As a man thinketh in his heart, so is he.*

- Take a few moments to absorb it, then apply it to yourself.

- Take note of your thoughts.

Did you go quickly to self-critical thinking—that your imperfect thoughts mean your heart isn't good? Maybe your thinking went something like this: "If that's true, then I'm a hopeless case" or "I have a lot of bad thoughts, so I must be a bad person. I'll never be good enough."

While you might think these thoughts would motivate you to do better, they actually create such negative feelings that they *de*motivate you. Rather than propelling you to work harder, they discourage you. They might even stop you from trying at all and thus from progressing. This does not mean that the phrase "I have a lot of bad thoughts" isn't true. It's the next thoughts—the conclusive judgments of yourself that you must be "bad" and will "never be good enough"—that are not true. It is the hardness and harshness of your thoughts *toward yourself* that are spiritually deadening, not thoughts that are true but spoken kindly, compassionately, and without final judgment.

About twenty years ago, my thoughts about the Proverbs scripture would have gone something like this: "Hmmm. I prefer 'As a *woman* thinketh in her heart, so is *she*.' Why can't the scriptures be more gender inclusive? I hate having to reword things in my mind so the scriptures really speak to *me*. Good heavens, Sue, you are so rigid. Can't you take your feminist glasses off for even five seconds? *These are the words of God!* How can you be so ungrateful?"

My self-berating would often become a loop, and my mood would plummet. To avoid that mood, I would close the scriptures and distract myself with some other activity. I sometimes would avoid the scriptures for long periods. Who wants to do something that triggers awful feelings about themselves? Even though I longed for the good feelings I also experienced when reading the scriptures, the discouraging feelings *created by my thoughts around my reading experience* were strong enough to make me avoid them. As a result, my spiritual growth was impeded.

I did not have the clarity then to realize that the scriptures themselves were not the problem, nor were my feminist ideas. Rather, the problem was my self-punishing thoughts that would escalate as I read. Getting this clarity—that it is our thinking that could use some adjustment and not necessarily the frustrating thing in front of us (though it could be that as well)—is a first step in gently leading ourselves away from perfectionism and toward a more rewarding path. I'm choosing carefully the words "our thinking could use some adjustment" rather than our thinking "must be transformed" or "has to be overhauled." *Adjustment* is enough for now. Again, words matter.

Today, my thoughts about the Proverbs scripture would go more like this: "There is such a deep truth in that. 'As *I* think in my heart, so am *I*.' Much of my inner life is good. I could do better, but I see progress, and I feel good about that."

NOTICE YOUR THOUGHTS[1]

Becoming aware of your self-injuring thoughts and replacing them with healing thoughts is a straightforward, relatively easy first step to alleviate some of the pain of perfectionism. Starting here will lay a solid foundation for the steps in following chapters. This might sound too simple and perhaps not sophisticated enough if you consider yourself already self-aware. But it is not. It works.

Begin by noticing your thoughts during the day. If you're like most busy people, you won't remember to do this very often at first. Keep trying, and you'll start to remember more. Pay attention to times when you feel anxious or worried about something that you're responsible for. Say, for example, that you're speaking or teaching a lesson in church in a few weeks, and you find your anxiety rising whenever you think about it. Notice your thoughts around the anxiety.

After a few days of taking mental notes, try writing down your thoughts. Write them down as they occur to you. Don't edit them or sugarcoat them. Here's an example:

SAMPLE THOUGHT JOURNAL

SITUATION	THOUGHTS AROUND SITUATION
Preparing a lesson or talk.	Last time I spoke, I saw people yawning and some heads nodding. I'm such a bore. What if that happens again? I have to get my lesson just right, like Brother Johnson's lessons always are.

	I need to get going on this sooner instead of putting it off until the last minute like I always do. Procrastinors are losers. Why don't I ever learn?
Thinking about asking a woman out for a date.	I'm such a bumbling idiot on the phone. What if she realizes that before I get two sentences out? I can't try this again until I feel fully confident.
Making an important decision.	I'm so scared to pray about this because I never get an answer. I must be unworthy or not sincere enough. Or maybe I'm just spiritually defective.

CREATE ALTERNATIVE WORDING

It's probably quite obvious how destructive the thoughts in the right-hand column are. While it's easy to recognize other people's self-injurious thinking, it's not as easy with ourselves. Most perfectionists are so used to thinking about themselves negatively that it's like the air we breathe—almost impossible to be aware of with any consistency. But we can get better at it with practice. Not perfect! But better.

Once you've begun to recognize, notice, and write down your own thoughts like the ones in the sample thought journal, you're ready to come up with alternative words and phrases. The objective is to find new wording that is gentle, kind, and compassionate.

Below are common words, phrases, and sentences that feed perfectionistic thinking. Alongside them are alternatives. There's space for you to write your own self-injuring words and alternatives. Come up with new phrases that are unique to you. Have fun with it.

Perfectionistic Words & Thoughts	Alternative Words & Thoughts
I should I must I've got to	I choose to I want to I don't want to I don't choose to I choose not to
Just right Exact Precise Absolute	Good enough Some good, some not as good Both wonderful and imperfect
Picture perfect	Lovely Wonderful
Flawless	Delightfully imperfect
Perfection	Progress
I always . . .	I sometimes . . .
I never . . .	I rarely . . .
I've got to get this lesson just right.	I would like this lesson to go well. The Lord can accomplish good with it no matter how it goes.
I've worked so hard to prepare, but I don't feel ready.	It's not possible to be completely prepared. What I've done is enough.
What if something goes wrong? Something always goes wrong.	Something might go wrong. If it does, I'll muddle through.
I worked so hard at that, but I know it wasn't my best. I've got to do better.	I can't do my best all the time. The Lord works with imperfect people always.

I have to be more exacting of myself. I've got to do my best. I should be further along by now. I should have known that.	I'm making progress. The Lord is helping me. Progress is good.
I can't be mediocre. I have to be the best at everything I do.	Average is okay. I'll save my best for what matters most. I'll let the Lord help me discern when my best is needed.

Perhaps you can hear relief in the words and sentences on the right. I see them as much closer to loving words the Savior would say to us.

Once you have your own replacement words and phrases, practice saying them to yourself and use them as often as you can. As they become more and more second-nature, you will find yourself feeling less anxious and more relaxed. Life is so much more enjoyable when we give ourselves permission to stop editing a piece of writing before it's perfect (which it will never be), to spend just a short time preparing a church lesson during a week with high demands, and to let go quickly when we make a poor decision.

This is not to say that exactness and precision do not have their place. We all want an exact dentist, not one who decides our new crown is "good enough." We're grateful for a surgeon whose incisions are precise, a mail carrier who gets the right mail to the right house, and a construction worker who will take the time to make excellent floors and walls. When it comes to working on becoming a better person, however, we hope our dentist, surgeon, mail carrier, and construction worker do not carry their exactness into their personal lives. In that arena, we hope they can be content with progression, not perfection—just as we have this hope for ourselves.

Enlisting Trusted Friends and Family in Your Journey

Many of your dearest friends and family might not know the extent of your internal struggles. They don't have access to your mind, so they might underestimate your distress. In any healing process, it's important to allow others in. Invite them to learn more about perfectionism. Tell them how it hurts you. Ask them how it might be hurting them. Risk a little and trust a lot. See chapter 5 for more information about how to do this.

NOTES

1.   For a straightforward, research-based discussion of thinking errors (or "cognitive distortions") common to perfectionists, see *When Perfect Isn't Good Enough*, by Martin M. Antony and Richard P. Swinson (Oakland, CA: New Harbinger Publications, 2009).

CHAPTER 3

Jessica's and Carlos's Trade-Ins

*J*essica, whom we met in chapter 1, had almost constant perfectionistic thoughts that made her anxious, depressed, discouraged, and distracted. She agreed to a keep a thought journal, focusing especially on her thoughts when she began to feel anxious about a situation coming up in the near future. Here's a sample from her journal:

JESSICA'S THOUGHT JOURNAL

SITUATION	THOUGHTS AROUND SITUATION
Preparing to attend church.	I have to be the prettiest one there.
	If I see someone prettier, I will be devastated.
	I shouldn't be so focused on appearance. I'm a total spiritual pygmy.

Seeing my sister's new house for the first time.	She shouldn't have a nicer house than me. I know I'm going to feel crazy jealous when I see it.
My children begging me to take them to the city swimming pool.	What if someone notices the cellulite on my thighs? If we saw someone from our ward, I would be completely humiliated. I really don't care how happy going to the pool makes my kids. I'm not taking them. I'm a selfish witch with a "b."

For Jessica, noticing these thoughts and recognizing their power to control her feelings—and her life—was a big step. It was not enough to just tell herself to stop the destructive thoughts; she needed replacement words and phrases. When she began to have thoughts at-the-ready to counter her self-berating thoughts, she began to make progress. Some of her replacement thoughts are explored below. They are only one possibility among many that she might have come up with.

• Instead of "I have to be the prettiest one there," *My worth goes much deeper than my appearance. I don't have to be the prettiest one there.* Jessica did not want to make this adjustment at first. Her sense of identity was so wrapped up in her beauty that to give up her original thought seemed like annihilation of her being. It was only when she tried saying the new thought to herself—despite her misgivings—that she understood its value. When she got a taste of the lowered anxiety, less discouragement, and more freedom the new thought gave her, she began to use it more consistently. Over time, she was able to believe the replacement phrases.

• Instead of "If I see someone prettier, I will be devastated," *If I see someone prettier, I will feel grateful I get another chance to refocus on my true value.* It also took a while for Jessica to accept that she could ever be indifferent, let alone grateful, to seeing a woman prettier than her. She didn't believe she could have that much power over her reactions. Over time, she began to accept that choosing the word devastated was at least partly creating those feelings. She could drop the word *devastated* and replace it with the word *grateful.* She began to cultivate gratitude for a number of things: that there is so much beauty in the world (not just hers!), that every time she sees a beautiful woman she has another opportunity to challenge her image-focused thoughts, that she can enjoy her attractiveness and not feel controlled by it. The more often she was able to say to herself, "I'm not devastated—I'm grateful," the more her feelings changed to match the words. *Changing her thoughts changed her feelings.* She was less anxious or depressed before an "exposure" event, during it, and after it. She was also more relaxed and peaceful.

As the positive feelings built, Jessica became less focused on herself and more present with her husband and children. She began to enjoy them more, and they enjoyed her more too. Eventually, she was able to stop nearly all comparisons and simply appreciate a pretty woman, whether she was "prett*ier*" or not.

• Instead of "I am a total spiritual pygmy," *I am a beloved daughter of God, and He loves me as I fumble my way toward greater spirituality.* Jessica, like many Latter-day Saints, knew how to tell herself Heavenly Father loves her, but she didn't necessarily feel it or believe it with much conviction. She knew she was supposed to believe it, but mostly she didn't. Words have power, and in this case it was helpful for her to say *aloud*, "I am a daughter of God, and He loves me." Speaking the words silently to herself wasn't nearly as effective. As she spoke them aloud frequently, she found they were like the seed in Alma's sermon about faith (Alma 42). Once planted, they bore the good fruits of peace and hope, and she wanted more.

It was also helpful to Jessica to see herself as fumbling and be okay with that—even with something as important as her spirituality. Spiritual growth does not happen in a straight line for anyone. It's more like a zigzagging upward climb. All of us experience our faith increasing at times but then have a setback and feel it decreasing. If we work through our experience, our faith increases again, often (but not always) stepping up to a higher level than before the setback.

We also have natural fluctuations in our spirituality that can't always be traced to a specific life circumstance. We simply feel more trusting of God and more in tune with the Spirit at some times than others. This ebb and flow is part of life, and it's okay.

CARLOS'S THOUGHT ADJUSTMENTS

Carlos also kept a thought journal. His perfectionistic anxieties focused around both anticipating perceived distressing situations and reviewing them obsessively after they occurred.

CARLOS'S THOUGHT JOURNAL

SITUATION	THOUGHTS AROUND SITUATION
Getting a C on a test.	Dad can never know about this. No son of his gets C's. People who get C's are worthless idiots.
Seeking personal revelation about an important decision.	I'm incapable of feeling the Spirit. Why even try? With billions of people in the world, Heavenly Father can't possibly care about me or my decision.
After an argument with his wife.	What would Dad think of my comebacks? Probably that I missed about 10 holes in her reasoning. I have to be right, or I'm nothing.

As Carlos looked over his journal, he began to recognize just how much his father's voice was still with him, even though he now lived hundreds of miles away. Pleasing this cold and critical man had consumed him as a child. When he became an adult and moved away, he had simply taken his father with him in his head. His defensive strategy to fend off criticism by making sure he did everything exactly right was adaptive in childhood, but now it was destroying his marriage, his sense of joy, and his ability to feel the Spirit.

"The Voice," as he called it—criticizing his performance, pointing out his flaws, questioning his motives—had become so habitual that it seemed automatic and involuntary. How could he change something so ingrained? He had already taken the first step by identifying the pattern. The next step was to replace The Voice with his own, more generous, voice.

• Instead of "People who get C's are worthless idiots," *I don't like getting C's, but they have nothing to do with my worth.* Acknowledging his upset feelings about a low grade was an important first step in dissipating Carlos's panic over this situation. Understanding that grades do not determine a person's fundamental value was just as important. Other thoughts that reassured him included: "This is not the end of the world" and "Getting a C is just a warning that I need to study a little harder for the next test" and "This is a difficult class—I'm grateful I'm going to pass it."

• Instead of "I'm incapable of feeling the Spirit," *I can feel the Spirit as I learn to allow my Heavenly Father into my heart.* It took time for Carlos to understand that when he prayed, he was praying to a berating, wrathful man—the image of his childhood father. He was listening for that critical voice to answer. He was bound to fail in his attempts to feel the Spirit because he was trying to tune into a spiritual frequency that doesn't exist. As Carlos searched the scriptures to find and begin to trust the loving, redeeming eternal Father and let Him supplant his earthly father, he felt liberated from his belief that God couldn't possibly care about him. Some of the scriptures that he allowed to penetrate his heart included:

"For God so loved the world . . ." (John 3:16)

"I have loved thee with an everlasting love . . ." (Jeremiah 31:3)

"I have graven thee upon the palms of my hands . . . I will not forget thee . . . (Isaiah 49:15–16).

• Instead of "I have to be right or I'm nothing," *I can be wrong and still be loved—both by my wife and by God.* Carlos didn't have to work on this one much because as he began to feel the Spirit and the Lord's love for him, arguments with his wife simply diminished. As he challenged his perfectionistic thoughts, he found he didn't need to be right in order to feel competent or loveable. In fact, he came to see that the more he tried to be right, the less loveable he acted. And when he saw—really saw—how his prideful comebacks wounded his wife, he no longer wanted to step into old power struggles with her.

CHAPTER 4

Setting Aside Stern Sayings

*A*side from the automatic thoughts we all have because of our life experiences, we also repeat to ourselves sayings that we've adopted for one reason or another. Some of us live by adages that our parents or teachers taught us were "gospel" truths. While all adages have truth in them, some can get perfectionists in trouble because we absorb anything around the idea of goodness in a super-serious way. Healing your perfectionistic pain may include recasting your personal slogans so that they serve you in your quest for progress rather than enslave you with their message that you have to try harder than is reasonable or realistic.

Here are some of the sayings that are especially hazardous for perfectionists.

- "A job isn't worth doing unless it's done well," and "Do it right or not at all."

In fact, lots of jobs are worth doing in a half-hearted, half-baked, "not right" way. A clean and organized garage, for example, is good to the point that you can find the things you need without wasting a lot of time.

A meticulously clean garage, however, takes a great deal of time that is better spent on other things. Non-perfectionists know this and instinctively ignore adages like these when they don't fit. Perfectionists, though, tend to apply them too widely and take them too far.

Jeanette, a young mother of two, had versions of these sayings pounded into her by both parents. She describes the effect on her life:

> For a while, doing something "perfect" became a handicap for me as I wouldn't want to even start a project or take the next step unless I had figured out how to do it perfectly without making a mistake the first time. I would over analyze for MONTHS until I figured out a way to do it and finally just did it. It usually wasn't as hard as I had made it out to be in my head, but I was so afraid to try because I didn't know how to do it right and if I couldn't do it right, I didn't want to do it at all.

A former Relief Society president, "Dina," describes how she would occasionally hear perfectionistic protests when she asked for compassionate service: "I can't help that sister. I am not close to her and don't approve of her lifestyle, so if I can't do it with all my heart and give freely in the right frame of mind then I just shouldn't do it at all." Dina eventually formulated a reply that helped these women set aside their unrealistic expectations and get down to work: "Sister, you can figure out your heart later. Right now this family needs our help."

John Henry Newman, a nineteenth-century British Cardinal in the Roman Catholic Church (who, incidentally, is being considered for official sainthood), said, "A man would do nothing, if he waited until he could do it so well that no one would find fault with what he has done."

Next time you embark on a job and this aphorism comes to mind, think instead:

> *I'll do a good enough job in most things and save my best for when it matters most. I will also accept that my definitions of "good enough" and "my best" won't be perfect.*

- "Never give up" or "Quitters never prosper" or "If at first you don't succeed, try and try again."

These adages are similar to the ones above. They're great when following them means you persist honorably and endure discomfort for a worthy goal. They're harmful when you persevere beyond what's reasonable.

When you refuse to move on despite the evidence that your investment won't return much, you risk foregoing other opportunities.

We perfectionists can take this persistence principle too far in small and simple things, such as practicing a piece of music ad infinitum or trying to perfect our three-point shot when we obviously have no knack for it. The consequences aren't usually dire in those cases. But when we take persistence too far in weightier matters, the consequences can be serious.

I lived by these adages to my detriment when I tried to break into screenwriting. Shortly after turning thirty, I moved to Los Angeles and began evening writing classes at UCLA. Within a few months I had completed my first script and became a finalist in a prestigious screenwriting contest. That got me a good agent and lots of encouragement—but not a sale. I decided I needed more structure to persist and was accepted into UCLA's full-time screenwriting program. Soon after, I won second place in an even more prestigious writing contest and got an even better agent. I accompanied a top Hollywood producer as we pitched my screenplay to every network and many cable companies. More hope but no sale.

I finished a third screenplay during the height of the "spec script" bidding wars in the early 1990s, when scripts written on speculation (rather than on assignment from a production company) began selling in high six figures and into seven figures. My agent predicted the bidding on my new script would begin at $750,000. I started looking at houses in Pacific Palisades. Again, though, no sale.

Those early near-successes kept me going until I had been in Los Angeles for eight years, still with lots of encouragement but no income from writing. I was making my living as a swing shift "document processor" at a large law firm so I could keep my days free for meetings with producers, directors, and writing groups. The meetings were getting fewer and father between, and the night-time work was becoming a terrible grind. I began to experience debilitating headaches, deep depression, and feelings of alienation from God, who I thought had directed me toward screenwriting. I hung in for three more years against the advice of those closest to me, no longer because I was still working hard at my goal but more because I could not accept failure and the blow to my image if I visibly gave up. Finally, burned out and with my emotional, spiritual, and physical health broken, I returned to Utah. I will never know what opportunities were lost or what health problems might never have been triggered had I not persisted beyond what was sensible and rational and moved on in another direction.

Burnout is a risk for anyone who is conscientious and persistent, but perfectionists go beyond persistent—and many of us specialize in burnout. We tend to do what pleases others and what keeps our image intact rather than what pleases us despite how others might see us. Often it's not that we're giving too much. It's that we're not giving out of our true desires but rather out of duty and image management. We press forward by force of will rather than by honorable passion or a deeper sense of what's right and good. Our motivation is coming from outside us rather than from inside us. We can't keep that up, and we burn out.

So instead of insisting that you will never give up no matter what, think instead:

> *I'll persist honorably and reasonably, and then I will move on. I might move on a little too soon or a little too late, but I can accept that my definition of "reasonably" won't be perfect.*

- "Practice Makes Perfect"

In truth, the vast majority of the time, no amount of practice ever makes perfect. Those who repeat this saying usually don't mean literally "perfect" but are expressing the valid idea that if you want to get good at something, you have work at it. For perfectionistic folks, however, these words can provoke anxiety and obsessive overpractice.

Think instead: *Practice makes progress.*

SUMMARY OF STRATEGY 1

Our thoughts are pivotal in who we are and how we feel about ourselves. Many of our thoughts are so automatic—seemingly programmed into our brains from an early age—that most of us are barely conscious of them. Making them conscious and replacing those that injure our spirits can powerfully heal our emotional and spiritual lives.

KEY POINTS:

- Your thoughts matter. They potently impact how you feel about yourself.

- You can change your thoughts and thus your feelings and moods.

- Keeping a thought journal can help you become more conscious of your thoughts, especially those that are distorted and self-injuring.

- You can replace harsh and judgmental thoughts with kinder, gentler thoughts.

- Enlist trusted friends and family in your healing process.

- Give this process time, and be patient with yourself.

- Your Savior is your ally. He is kind, merciful, and full of grace as you fumble your way toward becoming more like Him.

BREATHER

You Don't Have to Get It All at Once

I hope it's clearer to you now how damaging your self-critical thoughts are to your emotional and spiritual life. I hope it's also clearer how much power you have to adjust your thoughts and thus your feelings. As you begin to speak more kindly to yourself, be patient with yourself. You're not going to feel noticeably better within days—maybe within weeks, but more likely months. Again, *be patient with yourself.*

In years past, I often found myself feeling discouraged, sometimes even hopeless, about how slowly I was able to integrate gospel principles into my daily behavior. Then I discovered chapter 17 of 3 Nephi. Now when I feel the Lord must be angry with me because of my slow progress, I turn to these chapters. They describe the Savior preaching to the Nephites who were spared destruction after His crucifixion because they were more righteous. After He speaks to them for a while, He looks around and realizes they "cannot understand all [His] words." He doesn't chastise them or reprove them for their lack of understanding. There's no hint of anger or impatience. Rather, He is kind, merciful, and full of compassion. He says: "Go ye unto your homes and ponder upon the things which I have said, and ask of the Father, in my name, that ye may understand, and prepare your minds for the morrow, and I come unto you again" (3 Nephi 17:3).

If the more righteous part of the Nephites had trouble understanding the Savior's words when He was standing before them in the flesh, and yet He was kindhearted and empathetic toward them, how much more kind and empathetic will He be toward me when I lack understanding? When I don't get things right the first time, He will come to me again and again, patiently teaching me at a pace that is perfect for me.

What follows in this account is one of the most sacred and moving scenes in all of scripture. After offering His tender empathy, the Savior looks around again and sees that His listeners are in tears. They have fixed their eyes on Him, gazing intently, longingly, and He decides to stay a little longer. As He did in Jerusalem, He beckons to Him all the sick and "afflicted *in any manner.*" I can only presume that among those afflicted were the anxious, the discouraged, and the depressed who thought they were not good enough even though they had tried with all their might.

"And he did heal them every one." (3 Nephi 17:9)

As you seek to heal from your not-good-enough feelings, bring to mind these verses. In your moments of not understanding, not grasping, not getting it, your Savior will embrace you with kindness, compassion, and mercy. He wants you to do the same for others *and for yourself.*

STRATEGY TWO

Just Say No to the Comparison Trap

You've heard it a million times—don't compare yourself to others. Easier said than done. In this section, you'll learn:

- Effective replacement behaviors for comparing.

- Spiritual strategies to avoid comparing.

- How the Internet can increase your risk of toxic comparisons.

CHAPTER 5

Comparing Less and Sharing More

None of us is less treasured or cherished of God than another. . . . He loves each of us—insecurities, anxieties, self-image, and all. He doesn't measure our talents or our looks; He doesn't measure our professions or our possessions. He cheers on every runner. Walk peacefully. Walk confidently. Walk without fear and without envy. Be reassured of Heavenly Father's abundance to you always.

—Jeffrey R. Holland[1]

Latter-day Saints are a people with extraordinarily high standards and a lofty ultimate goal—exaltation. To know where we stand in our progress toward that goal, we frequently have to compare ourselves against what is required. This is where so many Latter-day Saints, and especially the perfectionistic among us, get into trouble. Because comparing ourselves to the standard of perfection can feel discouraging, we turn instead to comparing ourselves with other mortals. In recent years, we've been hearing a lot about this hazard from our Church leaders (and if your ward and stake are like mine, in talks and lessons). During the September 2011 general Relief Society meeting, President Dieter F. Uchtdorf said:

51

We spend so much time and energy comparing ourselves to others—usually comparing our weaknesses to their strengths. This drives us to create expectations for ourselves that are impossible to meet. As a result, we never celebrate our good efforts because they seem to be less than what someone else does.[2]

Elder Dean L. Larsen advised a BYU audience in 1986 to beware of comparing:

> One of the least profitable things we can do is to compare ourselves with others. Generally, when we make such comparisons, we match our weaknesses against the most prominent talents and virtues of those we admire or envy. No one comes out well in this useless game. Its effects can be devastating.[3]

And in 1990, then general Relief Society president Elaine Jack devoted much of her annual address to the dangers of comparing. She began by describing the "superwoman" fallacy many leaders have referred to over the years—the imaginary "practically perfect" Latter-day Saint woman who is fabulously competent at everything from baking bread to writing poetry while also being impeccably dressed and unremittingly in love with her righteous husband.

As women compare themselves to such a woman, President Jack said:

> I hear such comments as: "When they talk about being a good mother in Relief Society, I always feel so guilty because sometimes I shout at my children." "I'm not comfortable in church because my husband isn't active." "I wish I didn't have to work, but I need a paycheck to sustain my family." I've heard: "I'm not a mother. I'm not married, and I'm most painfully aware of this in Relief Society and sacrament meeting. I often go home feeling that they don't know what to do with me in the Church."[4]

It is not the reality of the challenges in these sisters' lives that is the problem. Facing reality and being realistic are good things. What is not helpful and can be so damaging to our spirits is to compare our overall goodness or value to the *external appearances* of other people's lives. As President Jack said, "We can never accurately take the measure of our lives based on social, economic, ethnic, age, marital, or physical conditions."[5]

External appearances are always incomplete representations of a whole and are almost always inaccurate, misleading, and deceptive. Using other human beings' outer picture to evaluate ourselves is like judging a family's home life by their home's curb appeal. A cozy-looking cottage could hide devastating conflict inside its walls. A dilapidated town house could belie loving relationships behind the front door. And all the possibilities in between.

An LDS blogger pinpointed astutely that one of the reasons we compare external observations is that they're easier to measure.

> I don't know that you can measure, "Today I was full of charity—check!" the way you can measure, "I always look fantastic," or "I was back to my pre-baby weight five weeks after the delivery." It's easier to shop at the right stores or see that your blog has the right design or gets so many comments. They provide validation or pat on the back. There are lots of ways that we can hope that we're successful or feel that we're successful, but that's not as visible as when you see someone with a new model of car, or living vicariously through their husband's fancy job, or whatever it might be.[6]

External appearances are also not what matters. It is our inner lives—our hearts, our diligence over time, who we are becoming—that matter. Taking the measure of ourselves in these things can be daunting too, but if done with self-compassion, the outcome is much more likely to be encouraging rather than discouraging.

The Antidote to Comparing: Sharing

So we know it's a good idea to compare less, but *how* do we do it? Can we really resist the impulse to look at an accomplished person and not tick down a list of what they have that we don't have? The answer is yes, of course. It might not be easy and you won't become perfect at it, but it is possible to improve.

It's easier to replace an old behavior with a new one rather than try to simply stop the old one. In this case, *sharing* can be a powerful replacement for comparing.

Sharing what?

Your vulnerabilities.

Say what? I'm a perfectionist who's deathly afraid someone will discover that I'm dumb or weak or flawed—and I'm supposed to share my dumbness or weakness or flawed-ness?

Yes.

The antidote lies in sharing your vulnerabilities. Let me explain.

Perfectionists are just like everyone else in their need to belong, to feel loved, and to love others. But we tend to be blind to the barriers we create against these longings. It's so ingrained in us that we have to be flawless to be loved that we don't even see that those very efforts to be flawless (or to project a flawless image) engender alienation—the opposite of what we want. When we allow others to see only the "perfect" parts of us (or what we hope looks perfect) and work hard at covering up our imperfectness, we present a false self to others. This mask of perfectness is a barrier between us and those we want closeness with. The more we guard against exposure of our flaws, the thicker the mask becomes and the less others are able to penetrate it and access our mask-less selves.

When we take off the mask of perfectness and allow others to see who we really are, including our flaws and the messiness of our lives, we open the door to intimacy and belonging. We might hope others will simply see beneath our masks so we don't actually have to take them off, but this hope yields only disappointment. We have to be the ones to remove our masks. No one can do that for us. When we let ourselves be vulnerable, we can enjoy the fruits of love and intimacy. When, in turn, we're in a more loving place and feel more belonging, we are happier and more peaceful.

The replacement behavior for comparing, then, is sharing our mistakes, blunders, weaknesses, faults, and need for help. When we feel ourselves revving up to cover a mistake or squash a desire to ask for help, we can choose instead to share the mistake or the need. While we might expect that exposing our weaknesses would make us feel worse, in fact it is healing. It's a relief to be authentic. And when others know we're hurting, they can help.

The Apostle Paul taught, "Confess your faults one to another, and pray for one another, that ye may be healed" (James 5:16).

The Relief Society president in my ward, Margo Newns, recently did this, and I share her experience here with her permission.

> About six months after being called as Relief Society president, I got to a point where my health and family time were being compromised, and I realized I needed help. I felt like a failure. I reluctantly made an appointment with my bishop. As I got ready to leave for his office, my husband, Jeremy, stopped me. He knows how hesitant I am to admit I can't do it all.
>
> "Are you going to ask for help?" he asked.

"Yes," I answered reluctantly. "I know I need help."

"But you like to *pretend* you don't need it, don't you?"

"Yes."

My husband was right. I like to think I'm superwoman, but I'm not and I don't need to be. I was never intended to do it alone. When I got home, Jeremy followed up and questioned if I had asked for help. It felt good to say that I had.

Shortly after the appointment, Margo took her willingness to be vulnerable a step further. She disclosed her feelings of being overwhelmed and needing help with the women in her ward during Relief Society. After the meeting, I thanked Margo for sharing her vulnerabilities and asked her if she would be willing to reflect further. She did, and a few days later wrote this:

> Just before I gave that lesson, someone asked me if I ever get overwhelmed. I was surprised she asked this because I feel overwhelmed all the time and thought others could tell. I told her yes and that before I could come to this meeting I had to say a prayer to get myself here. She was so relieved that she wasn't alone. This is one of the reasons I was willing to share that experience—so that others could learn from it and not get caught in the trap. I felt strongly if others could learn from this experience it would help them.
>
> We were never meant to get through this life alone. We are surrounded by others to help us. As I thought about how strongly I felt I should be able to do it all and how others need help more than me so I shouldn't ask for any, I started to study the scriptures about pride. I didn't like what I found. I am still learning, but my eyes have been opened to the concept that by not letting others help me, I am not progressing myself. We don't have to be perfect. We just need to be trying, and we need to be charitable to ourselves and to others. Perfection is a process that can only be completed when we are resurrected. We cannot do it alone—we must rely on the Savior.

Like Margo, Carlos (introduced in chapter 1) found relief in sharing his vulnerabilities. A few weeks into counseling, he began to acknowledge to his therapist that he almost constantly felt anxiety, fear, and shame. It was a new experience for him to reveal that he had any "negative" feelings. He told his counselor: "I have never shared these feelings and thoughts before. It's good to say them out loud and be able to trust someone with them."

A one-time sharing, of course, does not a non-perfectionist make. We become a recovering perfectionist when we're able to share our vulnerabilities regularly. It's not wise to do this with just anyone. Rather, first choose people you trust and feel safe with. As you begin to feel the relief of disclosure, risk a little here and there with people you aren't so sure are "safe." Generally I think you'll find that your vulnerability is safe with more people than you realize. Once in a while you'll be disappointed. You might pull back in a little after a disappointment, but don't stay there too long. Try again soon.

You cannot heal by yourself. You need others—both heavenly and human beings. Let your spouse, bishop, and friends into your struggles and allow them to accompany you on this journey.

On the Sunday that Margo shared her feelings, she had no way of knowing who in her audience would be receptive and who might think less of her. She took a big risk to so publicly bare her needs. The risk paid off.

> What a relief to let others know that I'm not perfect and that I'm weak and vulnerable. In admitting that I can't do it alone, I've been able to better see others' needs and help them through the process of accepting help. I've also found by admitting I have weakness I don't notice the weakness of others as much or am more understanding. What a great blessing that is.

Our Savior's Example

My final reason to persuade you that it's okay—even recommended—to share your vulnerabilities is the fact that Jesus Christ Himself did this very thing on at least three occasions during His mortal ministry. While His vulnerability was not the result of faults or sins, it was vulnerability nevertheless. I believe He wants us to follow Him in all he did, including being vulnerable.

First, in Gethsemane, He shared his fear as he prayed, "O my Father, if it be possible, let this cup pass from me" (Matthew 26:39). Second, while suffering on the cross, He shared his feelings of abandonment, "My God, my God, why hast thou forsaken me?" (Matthew 27:46) Was the Savior of the world, God Himself, truly vulnerable in that moment? Elder Jeffrey R. Holland said this: "The loss of mortal support He had anticipated, but apparently He had not comprehended this [loss of heavenly support]."[7]

And third, the Savior revealed his wounds to the Nephites. When appearing to them after His crucifixion, He said, "Arise and come forth unto me, that ye may thrust your hands into my side, and also that ye may feel the prints of the nails in my hands and in my feet" (3 Nephi 11:14). He then showed His wounds to all 2,500 men, women and children present. He did this first to witness to them that He had been slain for their sins. I believe He also did this to show them—and us—that we too should reveal our wounds to others. His wounds were physical, but they are a symbol of all human hurts and failings of every kind from the beginning of time throughout the centuries. Some of our wounds are self-inflicted through sin, but many of them are not. They are the result of human frailty or the sins of others.

The Savior invited the Nephites to not only see his wounds but also, in a most tender intimacy, to touch them. They are the "prints" of the nails in His hands and feet. Scars. He chose to show his *healed-over* wounds. They were not flaws but evidence of His suffering *and His healing*. They testify both of what He did for us and what the Father did for Him—and what together the Father and the Son can do for us. We can follow His example and share our wounds and scars as He did, judiciously and humbly. As we do, we can take further steps in our efforts to heal from perfectionism

NOTES

1. Jeffrey R. Holland, "The Other Prodigal," *Ensign*, May 2002.

2. Dieter F. Uchtdorf, "Forget Me Not," *Ensign*, November 2011.

3. Dean L. Larsen, "The Peaceable Things of the Kingdom," *New Era*, February 1986.

4. Elaine L. Jack, "These Things Are Manifested unto Us Plainly," *Ensign*, November 1990.

5. Ibid.

6. Admin., Mormon Women Project, "Seriously So Wise," Interview September 8, 2010, retrieved 7-3-2012 from http://mormonwomen.com/2010/09/08/seriously-so-wise.

7. Jeffrey R. Holland, "None Were with Him," *Ensign*, May 2009.

CHAPTER 6

Embracing the Panoramic View

Spiritual growth does not occur in a straight line, nor does it happen in giant leaps. It comes in small, sometimes almost imperceptible steps. If we assess our spiritual selves according to a snapshot of the present moment, we're likely to get a distorted and inaccurate picture. Perfectionists tend to take these snapshots when we've just fallen short (or think we have), giving us an especially skewed reality. It's after the priesthood blessing we gave to a home teachee that felt uninspired or after our family home evening was a chaotic disaster that we look at where we are and think it's all hopeless and sink into discouragement.

Remember (gently!) that as a perfectionist, you are prone to measuring yourself by your latest "performance." When you haven't lived up to an expectation, you're likely to see yourself as globally not good enough. To kindly coach yourself away from snapshots and toward the bigger picture, try these steps:

1. Recognize that assessing yourself after a performance can be valuable. Perfectionists tend to assess themselves more than

others, and in this case your propensity can serve you well—if you're able to assess without harsh judgment.

2. As you assess, gently remind yourself that whatever the result of your assessment, this is one blip along a lengthy timeline.

3. Whether you believe you did well or not, avoid overplaying the importance of the moment.

4. Honestly review your overall progress and place this single performance in long-term perspective.

5. Remember that *even when the stakes are very high, if your intentions are good, any single poor performance will not have an eternal consequence.*

You might not believe the words in italics, but allow me to persuade you with a worst-case scenario based on a composite of several real-life incidents.

Suppose you home teach a widowed woman with three small children. You and your companion diligently serve your assigned family and grow to love this mom and her children. One evening, the three-year-old girl is hit by a car, and you rush to the emergency room. You arrive and find the child in critical condition. Her mother asks you to give her daughter a priesthood blessing. You do so, and you feel inspired to say that the child will be healed and live a normal life. But she dies.

The mother, of course, is devastated. And so are you, both because of the terrible loss of a precious child you love and because of your mistaken blessing. Not only was it apparently uninspired, but it is now complicating the grief and heightening the pain for the bereaved.

This experience would be devastating for any priesthood holder. For a man with perfectionistic tendencies, it could be disastrous. A failure at something of such great consequence could derail you for a long time— even a lifetime. But it doesn't have to. You have the power to make even the worst of your performances serve you in your desire to spiritually progress, one step at a time.

1. *Recognize that assessing after a performance is valuable.* You're going to assess this experience over and over again, and that's normal. You could hardly do otherwise. Let your reflective powers serve you as you move through the next steps.

2. *Gently remind yourself that this is one blip along a lengthy time-line.* As long-term as the negative effects of this situation might appear, they need not be eternally negative. All experiences, and especially those where our hearts were in the right place—*even if our heart misguided us and resulted in something that seems awful*—can be turned to our good if we invite the Lord into the process.

3. *Don't overplay the failure.* You might ask—Is that even possible in this situation? Isn't it more likely that I'll run for cover, hide, and *underplay* it? That's possible, yes, but perfectionistic tendencies are more likely to cause you to catastrophize. But isn't this, in fact, a catastrophe? No, it isn't. The errant blessing was the result of human weakness, not sin—and it was rooted in love and hope (and perhaps anxiety). Those factors overwhelmed your senses and kept you from hearing God's will. It happens to many, many people. It is not talked about often for at least two reasons: first, because it is so hard to look at squarely, let alone talk about honestly; and second, because no one wants to risk diminishing the faith of others. But, as I wrote in my introduction, whenever we gloss over distressing experiences in our desire to appear more perfect than we are, we lose a chance to deepen and mature our faith. This is a chance for you—and for the family you home teach—to do exactly that.

How might that be accomplished? Here's one possible approach.

First, write down what happened and your feelings about it. On the left-hand side of your paper, simply list all your thoughts and feelings, no matter how extreme. Then list all the bad things that you think might happen to each of the family members you home teach because of this experience. Put your list away for a few days or a week, then get it out and look it over. On the right-hand side, write what you think the Savior would say in response to each thought and feeling. Do this *slowly* and *prayerfully.* Meet with your bishop to go over your before and after lists, and listen carefully to his counsel.

Once your list feels more inspired rather than reactive, draft a short scenario of how you might approach the family you home teach. If you enlist the Spirit and do this exercise with reasonable thoroughness, there will be surprises. Finally, muster your courage and meet with the family. At this point, you will know roughly what to do and say.

As you go through this process, it might also be helpful to recall the comforting words of Dallin H. Oaks:

> Like most who officiate in healing blessings, I have often struggled with uncertainty on the words I should say. For a variety of causes, every elder experiences increases and decreases in his level of sensitivity to the promptings of the Spirit. Every elder who gives a blessing is subject to influence by what he desires for the person afflicted. Each of these and other mortal imperfections can influence the words we speak.[1]

COMPARE YOUR PRESENT SELF TO YOUR PAST AND FUTURE SELF, NOT YOURSELF TO OTHERS

We're each on our own, distinctive version of the path toward eternal life. We start on it from different places and at different times in our lives and with different navigation skills. We move along it at varying speeds. Some have more godly people around them to help them along the way. Some have fewer. Most of us have at least some hindering family, friends, and other circumstances. Some have many. If we've come from a difficult childhood and just commenced on the path and then compare ourselves to a person who came from a loving home and started on the path much earlier, we are bound to find ourselves lacking. The Lord does not do this. He knows where we came from and the factors that limit our agency. Can you imagine Him comparing a spiritually disadvantaged person to a spiritually privileged one? He does not do this.

It's so easy to forget how damaging comparisons can be and turn our attention to people who are the best examples of what we're trying to achieve—setting ourselves up for discouragement and despair. As deeply as we might know that comparing ourselves to others can be damaging, we do it anyway.

We know it would be better to compare ourselves to the ideal of Jesus Christ, but He is a more subtle presence. He does not speak in sacrament meeting or personally deliver a gospel doctrine lesson. His human brothers and sisters do that. Without much effort, we can hear them audibly, see them with our human eyes, and touch them with a handshake or hug. They are easily and instantly accessible in a mortal way that our Savior is not. We can all too easily look to them to take the measure of our value, worth, and worthiness. As we choose these standards against which we measure ourselves, it's natural to choose the mortals who *appear* to have it all together.

To get a clearer picture of what we're doing when we compare ourselves to others' external appearances, consider this scenario. You've just heard Sister Chang give an amazing gospel doctrine lesson about the Atonement. She seems to "get it" in a way you think you never will. You feel discouraged by that, so you go to the Lord in prayer and ask Him to help you understand the Atonement like Sister Chang does.

But the goal is not to be more like Sister Chang. It's to understand the Atonement better as *you* need to given your individual circumstances and mission. So a more helpful approach would be to study and to pray for help understanding what the Atonement means and how to apply it to your life. Instead of using Sister Chang's lesson to beat yourself up, you could use it to compare *your current self to your past self and to your possible better self.*

Chances are good that you understand the Atonement now better than you did two, ten, or forty years ago. When you feel pangs of comparison with others, recall *your* path of growth and evolvement. Even if your comprehension has expanded only a little, value that expansion and express gratitude for it. As you recognize the steps you have already taken, it will be easier to feel hope that you can take further steps. Ponder how you might continue to grow. Pray for help as you formulate a step or two that will lead you in that direction. Perhaps dedicate the next few months of sacrament time to this purpose. At the end of those few months, take stock again. Chances are good that your understanding has grown. If it hasn't, try again—with gentleness and kindness toward yourself.

As you look back and see progress, use that evidence to trust in your ability to continue enlarging your soul and becoming more like Christ. As you're kind and patient with yourself, just as your Savior is kind and patient with you, this process will become easier.

NOTES

1. Dallin H. Oaks, "Healing the Sick," *Ensign*, May 2010, 49–50.

CHAPTER 7

Replacing Comparison with Gratitude

The Lord is good to all: and his tender mercies are over all his works.

Psalm 145:9

For me, gratitude has become the closest thing to magic that I know. It is a most amazing principle. Many years ago, when I was in the depths of despair about not finding an eternal companion, my mother tried to tell me to start a gratitude practice. I was dismissive of the idea. I'm supposed to be grateful in the midst of this unbearable deprivation? Grateful for a life that feels lesser compared to everyone around me? What do I have to be grateful for that could possibly make up for the lack of a companion and children? For a long time, her suggestion ticked me off.

A few years later, several tenderizing factors entered my life that helped me compare less and choose gratitude instead. They loomed so large that I could not ignore them. Their entrance had nothing to do with any effort on my part—they were pure tender mercies.

One was a dog. I had never had a dog in my life and knew nothing about them. I had just moved from an urban area of Los Angeles to

Utah to recover from a serious case of burnout and depression. The back window of my new home looked out onto a greenway about the length of three football fields. At the end of the greenway, I could see a dot-sized dog inside a small dog run. He rarely got out, and his captivity gnawed at me. I think now that his situation mirrored mine in a strange and wonderful way. I had never met the neighbor who owned the dog, but something compelled me to knock on his door and ask to meet his dog. He looked puzzled but said okay. Rex, it turned out, was a large, depressed, anxious, and needy four-year-old German wirehaired pointer. I told the owner I was ill and trying to walk more and asked if I could take Rex with me as motivation. He looked at me like I was from Mars, shrugged his shoulders, and said okay.

After our first walk, during which I felt like my arm was going to be torn from its socket, I tried to return Rex to his kennel. But he resisted. He liked freedom with a pushover human. I shoved his back end to get him to go in, and he reeled around and bit me on the thigh. My jeans kept his teeth from breaking the skin, and I found myself feeling shocked that I didn't care he had just bit me. Inexplicably, I wanted to be with this dog. A few days and a few walks later, I introduced Rex to my father, and Rex tried to bite him. I thought then that I really ought to stop hanging around with this aggressive canine. But I didn't. Instead I researched dog behavior and discovered that Rex's aggression indicated fear and anxiety. So I loved him up. After three weeks of regular walks and lots of affection, his true temperament emerged—loving and sweet. He never made an aggressive move again.

For the next eight months, I walked Rex every day and sometimes twice a day. He could see me from afar as I approached, and he would leap and bark with joy. As I walked him, I got to know my neighbors, especially the children, who all wanted to pet him and help me with his care. My depression began to lift. Rex's exercise needs were high, and I found myself taking him into fields and canyons to let him run free. He led me on adventures that had me chasing him into irrigation canals, searching for him in cornfields with skunks, removing a deer carcass so he would stop rolling in it day after day, and twice failing dog obedience classes. For Rex, I had to get out of the house and engage in life—a dog's life, at least—and my depression lifted further. And I fell in love. With a dog. I adored him with a fierce love that I didn't know was possible between humans and animals.

After eight months, Rex's owner decided to move to a condo where he couldn't have a pet. He decided to sell Rex to a hunting club, but he told me I could have him if I would pay what the hunting club would pay. I was willing, but others in my home vetoed adding a dog to the household. Even worse than the thought of Rex not being in my life was the thought that he would be without a family and could be poorly treated. I couldn't bear it. I desperately tried to find him a good home somewhere, but no one was interested. I panicked and despaired. This could not happen to my Rex. But I could not take him, and moving was not an option.

Time was running out. The day before Rex was scheduled to be carted off, a neighbor called and asked me to come over. I did, and he and his wife invited me to sit on their couch.

"We hear it's your birthday," they said.

"Yes," I said.

"We have a present for you."

I gave them a puzzled look.

"We know how much you love Rex. We have space for him in our backyard, and you can keep him here. You'll be responsible for him, but he can stay here as long as you need him to."

I was speechless. Was I hearing right? Yes. Were they sure? Yes.

The tragedy of permanent separation was averted. Rex was mine.

My heart overflowed with gratitude. How could I possibly disregard this remarkable tender mercy? How could I refuse any longer to see my life as blessed?

After three months with his doghouse at the rescuing neighbor's yard (but mostly at my side), Rex became a full-time resident at my home. He became beloved by all. For eight more years, he would be adored by dozens of people, blessing me and all who knew him with his loving nature. When he died just short of thirteen, by then in a different house complete with doggy door and large fenced backyard chosen just for him, neighbors grieved along with me and helped me honor him with a memorial service.

Rex was sent to me by a loving Heavenly Father who knew my heart was hardening and knew the exact thing it would take to soften it. He was one of many of the Lord's tender mercies that unfolded over time, bringing me back to myself and back to him. But it was Rex who opened my heart to *seeing* the other tender mercies as they came along—and the ones that were always there. As I was increasingly able to recognize my blessings, my ability to feel grateful grew. The more I expressed my gratitude to my Heavenly Father, the more blessings I saw. Now, at age fifty-five, still without companion or children or grandchildren, I view my life as rich and full and amazingly blessed. My mother, as always, was right.

Situations still arise that tempt me to compare myself to others, especially occasions like my friends' children's weddings, missionary farewells, and grandchild baby blessings. When they come up, I consciously and intentionally turn away from comparison and toward gratitude. It works almost every time. (It's not that the principle *can't* work every time. It's that an imperfect human being can't make perfect use of a good principle every time. And that's okay.)

Gratitude is no longer a technique I grab on to when I feel down. It isn't ticking down a list of my blessings to make myself feel better. It is, rather, *a way of being.* As Amulek urged his listeners, we can "live in thanksgiving daily, for the many mercies and blessings which he [God] doth bestow upon you" (Alma 34:38). When we have this "spirit of gratitude in our hearts," as Elder Quentin L. Cook said, we're able to be grateful even for blessings we don't know we have.[1] Gratitude as a way of being (as opposed to listing blessings) is a powerful antidote to perfectionism because it steers us away from feelings of inadequacy, unworthiness, and "not-good-enough-ness" toward truly *seeing* that we are adequate, worthy, and enough. Our blessedness becomes irrefutable evidence.

The author of *Attitudes of Gratitude*, M. J. Ryan, claims that gratitude cures perfectionism. I wouldn't go that far, but I agree with her that gratitude is a potent factor in recovery. Here's her lovely description for what it can do:

> When we pour the oil of appreciation for life in all its imperfections over our experience, we ourselves can't help but be anointed. Suddenly seized by joy for the crazy, mixed-up world, we recognize ourselves as part of that world, and take our rightful place as a child of the Universe, perfectly acceptable in all our imperfection.[2]

CARLOS'S GRATITUDE

Carlos, whom we met in chapter 1, knew he was supposed to be grateful and went through the motions of expressing gratitude here and there, but he didn't *feel* grateful. He and his counselor decided it might help for him to focus more intently on the feelings. For one week, he devoted all his prayers to gratitude only. He didn't ask the Lord to bless others or to bless him with anything except for one thing—the ability to feel grateful. At the end of that week, his feelings hadn't changed. He decided to keep trying. Within a few weeks, grateful feelings began to swell.

As Carlos continued working on noticing his blessings and expressing gratitude for them, his ability to feel grateful became more consistent. As time went on, Carlos's perspective about his demanding and critical father began to change. Where before Carlos had seen only his father's negative traits, he began to see—and feel grateful for—his father's positive traits. He had almost forgotten that it was his father who had taught him to love music, culture, and science—things that added so much joy to his life. As he felt grateful to his father for passing on these precious values, his feelings of anger and resentment began to dissipate. As they diminished, he began instead to feel his father's pain. His father was a perfectionist too, but he didn't have the resources to heal as Carlos did. In a beautiful upward spiral, his bitterness transformed into compassion, which in turn helped him build even more gratitude.

IDEAS FOR YOUR OWN GRATITUDE PRACTICE

To integrate gratitude into your life, not just count blessings, here are some ideas.

- At regular intervals, say a gratitude prayer—one where you don't express anything but gratitude. Ask the Lord to help you see blessings you aren't aware of.

- Keep a "tender mercies" journal. Look back on your day for the hand of God in your life. Elder Henry B. Eyring reports that he did this "for years." He recalls: "As I kept at it, something began to happen. As I would cast my mind over the day, I would see evidence of what God had done for one of us that I had not recognized in the busy moments of the day. As that happened, and it happened often, I realized that trying to remember had allowed God to show me what He had done."[3]

- Commit to being grateful. Leading gratitude researcher Robert A. Emmons, professor of psychology at the University of California-Davis, says studies show that "making an oath to perform a behavior increases the likelihood that the action will be executed." He suggests that you "write your own gratitude vow, which could be as simple as 'I vow to count my blessings each day,' and post it somewhere where you will be reminded of it every day."[4]

- Set aside a few minutes during family meal times for each person to express what he or she is grateful for.

- As you consider what you're grateful for, be okay with also expressing what you're *not* grateful for. If you're not grateful for the way your wife snapped at you, then you can recognize an opportunity to be forgiving (and be grateful for that!). Seeing the shadows in your life is not being ungrateful. It's being whole.

- If you miss a day in your gratitude practice, so what? Don't expect perfection and be forgiving of yourself.

NOTES

1.   Quentin L. Cook, "The Songs They Could Not Sing," *Ensign*, November 2011, 105.

2.   M. J. Ryan, *Attitudes of Gratitude: How to Give and Receive Joy Every Day of Your Life* (New York: MJF Books, 1999), 30.

3.   Henry B. Eyring, "O Remember, Remember," *Ensign*, November 2007.

4.   Robert Emmons, "10 Ways to Become More Grateful," posted November 10, 2010 to the website "The Greater Good: The Science of a Meaningful Life," retrieved July 2, 2012 from http://greatergood.berkeley.edu/article/item/ten_ways_to_become_more_gratefull.

CHAPTER 8

Limiting Exposure to Gleaming Online Content

$\mathcal{W}$e all know the Internet is both a wonderful resource and a minefield of hazards. For perfectionistic Latter-day Saints, especially women, the Internet can be particularly risky. Photos, stories, and messages women encounter on blogs, Facebook, and Pinterest can overwhelm the senses with alluring but highly unrealistic messages. With their glossy take on real life, perfection-oriented websites can become a form of porn for females. While the images are not lewd, they arouse a materialistic lust for the objects of our desire and create a fragmented portrait of others that distorts their wholeness and warps our perspective of reality. The images can be addictive and may create unworkable expectations of home, family life, and husbands. When these expectations are not met, depression can follow. Like pornography, these sites can become an unhealthy escape (rather than respite) from working out the thorny challenges of real life. These effects are all as anti-family, anti-gospel, and anti-Christlike living as pornography.

The creator of a blog that parodies the "perfect" young, married Mormon life addressed the pressure to be perfect in an online archive of interviews with Mormon women. Her blog (discontinued in 2011, but all posts remain online) was called *Seriously So Blessed*, and she wrote it anonymously. She said in the interview, also anonymously:

> In any highly homogeneous culture, we all feel pressure to be and look and think and act a certain way. Many Mormon women are hard on themselves because they're good and want to be good, and in our culture we do a lot of self-reflection and introspection on how we can improve. Part of being a member of the Church and part of being a person of faith and a follower of Christ is always thinking of how you can get better. With a lot of young American Mormon women that quest can get out of hand quickly. You start to think you need to be absolutely perfect in every area. You need to be having nonstop fun all the time, your marriage needs to be perfect, your kids need to be perfect, and you need to have pictures of every activity. I get emails from readers saying that there's this unattainable standard that they see people around them portraying (or seeming to portray) and that the blog helps them realize that nobody's perfect and it sounds ridiculous if you make things seem perfect all the time.[1]

These opportunities for comparison are abundantly available on Facebook, blogs, and sites like Pinterest. I have Yahoo as my home page so I can glance at headlines several times a day. A regular headline is some sort of tacky comparison between two female celebrities' appearance. (I have yet to see a comparison of male celebrities.) In a period of just a few weeks, these three headlines and teasers appeared:

- "Megan Fox in same outfit as teen star—The actress looks great in a glitzy skirt, but a young starlet manages to outshine her. (4-20-12)"

- "J. Lo's style overshadowed by actress—The star wears a daring dress months after another celebrity wears it better. Compare their looks. (5-6-12)"

- "Pipp's second-place fashion finish to sis"—Pippa Middleton can't quite measure up in a version of sister Kate's iconic blue engagement dress. (5-28-12)"

While these are direct comparisons that foster distorted thinking about appearance, sites like Facebook and Pinterest also create abundant opportunities for comparison. But you don't have to accept them. I regularly engage self-talk so I can enjoy the upsides of the web and minimize the downsides.

For example, on a single day on my Facebook newsfeed in 2012, posts included adorable photos of two friends' new grandbabies, glowing reports of three friends' exotic travels, the radiant photo of a friend and her husband celebrating their anniversary, and descriptions of gourmet meals a friend recently prepared. During the same twenty-four hours, friends posted about getting one hour of sleep because of sick kids, the angst of mid-life crisis, a funeral, and the disadvantages of being left-handed. Plus lots of inspirational quotes and photos.

If I chose to, I could focus on the shiny posts and feel envious, covetous, bitter, underprivileged, and depressed. Or I could focus on how I got eight hours' sleep the night before, my midlife crisis is behind me, I get my share of travel, and I can cook very well (if not gourmet). *Or*—I could simply enjoy the variety of experiences and advice and inspirational material and be grateful I have such a diversity of friends. I almost always choose the last option. Sometimes I get caught in brief envy, but mostly I have learned to feel gratitude for my friends' good fortunes as well as my own. The key is to recognize that we have a choice about how to react, whatever stimulus comes our way.

Valuing differences is also a powerful antidote to comparing. Rather than exclusively exposing yourself to websites that gloss over the realities of life, include in the mix websites that remind you how diverse the Mormon community is. One of the most compelling of these is the Mormon Women Project, an ongoing collection of articles about Mormon women from all walks of life. The variety of choices and challenges among these women, all of whom are striving to live the gospel, can warm the heart and help us feel we belong, no matter how "different" we think we are.

In a *Deseret News* article in March 2011, Mormon Women Project founder Neylan McBaine said she started the website with "the social goal . . . to debunk some myths of what it means to be a Mormon woman."[2]

Another source of imperfect but striving Latter-day Saints is the Church's "I Am a Mormon" series. At http://mormon.org/people/find, you can select the gender and age group of people you'd like to hear from and even their ethnicity or previous religion. You will find a fair number of happy-only profiles, but you'll also find stories of ordinary people from every walk of life struggling and striving.

NOTES

1.   Admin, Mormon Women Project, "Seriously So Wise," Interview September 8, 2010, retrieved 7-3-2012 from http://mormonwomen.com/2010/09/08/seriously-so-wise.

2.   Hadfield, Emily, "Mormon Women Project Profiles Rich Diversity of LDS Women," *The Deseret News*, March 7, 2011, retrieved 7-3-2012 from http://www.deseretnews.com/article/705368126/Mormon-Women-Project-profiles-rich-diversity-of-LDS-women.html?pg=all.

SUMMARY OF STRATEGY 2

*C*omparing ourselves to others can be devastating to our spirits. We can gently replace our tendency to compare with sharing our vulnerabilities, embracing the big picture, making our own progress the only point of comparison, and expressing gratitude.

KEY POINTS:

- Comparing seems so natural that sometimes we miss how harmful it can be.

- Reducing comparisons as best we can is healing.

- Sharing our vulnerabilities is a powerful antidote to comparing.

- Allowing trusted loved ones to accompany you on your healing journey is wise and helpful.

- Comparing our previous selves to our current selves and our current selves to our potential future selves can help us see progress.

- Being intentional about how we use the Internet can help us reduce comparing.

- As we learn these ways of becoming less perfectionistic, we can be caring and patient with ourselves.

BREATHER

Comforting Thoughts from Church Leaders

*H*ere are reassuring words our leaders have given us to help us remember our mortal goodness and our eternal identity. Let them sink in and comfort your soul.

"You are closer to heaven than you suppose. You are destined for more than you can possibly imagine."[1]

"Every one of us is more beloved to the Lord than we can possibly understand or imagine."[2]

"Each time I meet with the sisters of the Church, I sense that I am in the midst of . . . remarkable souls. I am grateful . . . for who you are: treasured daughters of our Heavenly Father with infinite worth."[3]

"The Savior's arms of mercy are always extended to each of us."[4]

"[T]he Savior's Atonement provides lifeboats for everyone. For those who think the trials they face are unfair, the Atonement covers all of the unfairness of life."[5]

"Thank you, my brothers and sisters, for the goodness of your lives. I thank you for your efforts in trying to measure up to the very high standards of this, the Lord's Church."

NOTES

1. President Dieter F. Uchtdorf, "Forget Me Not," *Ensign*, November 2011.

2. Elder Robert D. Hales, "Waiting upon the Lord: Thy Will Be Done," *Ensign*, November 2011, 71.

3. President Dieter F. Uchtdorf, "Happiness, Your Heritage," *Ensign*, November 2008, 117.

4. Randall K. Bennett, "Choose Eternal Life," *Ensign*, November 2011, 100.

5. Elder Quentin L. Cook, "The Songs They Could Not Sing," *Ensign*, November 2011, 106.

6. Gordon B. Hinckley, "This Glorious Easter Morn," *Ensign*, May 1996.

STRATEGY THREE

Nurture Your Spirituality

You can heal from perfectionism to a degree with cognitive techniques, willpower, friendship, love, and self-control. You'll do much better at those things if you enlist your Savior in your efforts. With His redeeming power, you'll also reach a deeper and more enduring healing.

In this section, you will find help

- Letting your Savior further into your heart and into your healing.

- Repenting without getting bogged down in perfectionistic hazards.

- Letting go of perfectionistic expectations about feeling the Spirit and receiving answers to prayers.

- Creating personalized strategies for handling scriptures that stir up your perfectionistic anxieties.

- Being still so you can hear your own voice and the voice of the Lord.

- Embracing yourself no matter how far short you think you fall.

CHAPTER 9

Receiving Jesus Christ as Your Ally

*T*hroughout these pages so far, I've interspersed ideas about how our Savior can help us become less perfectionistic. I've delayed a chapter dedicated to that topic because I'm hoping the previous chapters will help you become more receptive and open to the ideas I want to communicate now.

As I was growing up, I developed a sense that God is sort of like a super-vigilant policeman. I saw Him as watching and waiting to catch me in the slightest infraction and mete out punishment accordingly. My parents were not like this, so this way of thinking didn't come from them. For a while, I tried to retrace how I came to perceive God this way, but that search was fruitless. Now I simply acknowledge that my thoughts and feelings did develop along those lines and that tracking down where they came from isn't important. It *is* important to keep in mind that I still have a tendency to go toward that attitude, especially when I'm stressed or feeling guilty about something.

Because my perfectionistic filter was in place from an early age, it took time for me to recognize that comforting scriptures mostly passed through while harsher scriptures remained more prominent in my memory and tainted my understanding of life. Passages like this one in Ezekiel would stick with me: "As I live, saith the Lord God, surely with a mighty hand, and with a stretched out arm, and with fury poured out, will I rule over you" (20:33). Others included Genesis 6:17, where the Lord said He would bring a flood "to destroy all flesh," 2 Nephi 5:21, where the Lord cursed those who rebelled against Him, and Doctrine and Covenants 19:15, where the Lord commanded us to repent "lest I smite you by the rod of my mouth, and by my wrath, and by my anger, and your sufferings be sore—how sore you know not, how exquisite you know not, yea, how hard to bear you know not."

Verses that spoke of God's love and compassion filtered right on through and out of my memory. My view that God must be vengeful and angry made effective prayer almost impossible. I prayed consistently, but rather than listening for answers, I mostly got up off my knees quickly, afraid to hear back from the severe Father I perceived in my mind.

As I've talked to others about how they view God and their relationship with him, I've found my childhood paradigm surprisingly common among both Latter-day Saints and those of other faiths. It's especially common among perfectionists. So please know that if you can relate to these feelings, you're not alone.

Over time, I began to recognize what I was doing and tried to comfort myself with the idea that God the Father is harsh but that Jesus Christ is kind and gentle. I then began to distance myself from scriptures that talked about God's anger toward the wicked (me) and drew closer to Jesus's more gentle approach during His mortal ministry in the Holy Land and His post-crucifixion ministry in Bountiful. That made my spiritual efforts less anxiety-provoking—until I realized my tactic was doctrinally incorrect. My new way of thinking was as flawed as the original. I was quite shocked and mightily disappointed when it dawned on me that the angry God of the Old Testament and of the Doctrine and Covenants and of the Book of Mormon is in fact Jehovah—Jesus Christ. I also had to face the fact that God the Father and Jesus Christ are one in purpose and completely unified. One is not "more" of this or "less" of that.

With increasing awareness of my filter and efforts to modify it, over time I have come to view both God the Father and Jesus Christ as loving beings who love me individually and exquisitely. That doesn't mean I don't still have trouble *feeling* their love for me. I do. I'm a recover*ing* perfectionist, not a recover*ed* one. My difficulty did not come from overly demanding and controlling parents, as Elder Larry Y. Wilson so lovingly acknowledged is the case with many such children who develop perfectionism. He calls it a "tragic side effect of unrighteous dominion" and continues that he has "known some people who were subject to demanding and controlling leaders or parents, and they have found it hard to feel the very love from their Heavenly Father that would sustain them and motivate them along the path of righteousness."[1]

Whether you have a "policeman" view of God or not, I offer in this chapter several ways we all can further allow our Savior into our hearts and make Him central to our individual journeys toward eternal life.

What It Means to Receive

Because we perfectionists are all about doing our utmost to make things happen the way we think they should—including bringing about our own "celestialness"—being submissive or passive is anathema. We're not open to ideas around receiving because we associate them with being lazy and not sufficiently self-reliant. Healing from perfectionism comes as we shift our thinking about this.

Receive is a curious word. In common use, it often means simply getting something, such as *receiving* a letter in the mail. With that meaning of *receive*, we haven't done anything active except to open our mailbox. This kind of receiving is basically a passive act.

Many spiritual blessings in our lives are similarly sent to us without us having to do anything. Some of us, for example, are born with an unusually attuned sensitivity to the Spirit. Others are born to goodly (though imperfect) parents. Some spiritual gifts can be developed with effort, but to begin with they just *are*.

None of these ways of receiving requires much of anything from us. They're gifts, like a ribboned package appearing on our kitchen table. In this sense, we don't even necessarily have a choice about whether we "receive" them or not.

When we *choose* to receive spiritual things in a way that more overtly engages our agency, however, our spirits can progress in ways that passive reception does not allow. Receiving in this sense is both passive and active. It's passive in the sense that something valuable is being offered, and we don't have to do anything to qualify for the offer itself. It's active in the sense that we have to act to *make use* of the gift that's being offered.

We begin to actively spiritually receive when we recognize that an offer is being made. Elder David A. Bednar discussed this:

> Nephi teaches us, "When a man speaketh by the power of the Holy Ghost the power of the Holy Ghost carrieth [the message] unto the hearts of the children of men" (2 Nephi 33:1). Please notice how the power of the Spirit carries the message unto but not necessarily into the heart. A teacher can explain, demonstrate, persuade, and testify, and do so with great spiritual power and effectiveness. Ultimately, however, the content of a message and the witness of the Holy Ghost penetrate into the heart only if a receiver allows them to enter. Learning by faith opens the pathway into the heart.[2]

Elder Gerald R. Lund also emphasized this sacred *choice* each of us has in a talk called "Opening Our Hearts": "Let us make it a part of our everyday striving to open our hearts to the Spirit. Since we are the guardians of our hearts, we can choose to do so. We choose what we let in or hold out. Fortunately the Lord is anxious to help us choose wisely."[3]

Once we're aware that we're being offered a sublime gift, it's up to us to accept it or not. The scriptures and quotes below remind us that our Savior continually opens up His arms to help us—if we'll let Him. It's good for perfectionistic folks like us to read these words slowly, ponder them, and let them sink in.

- "Behold, he sendeth an invitation unto all men, for the arms of mercy are extended towards them." (Alma 5:33)

- "The Savior's arms of mercy are always extended to each of us."[4]

- "Yea, verily I say unto you, if ye will come unto me ye shall have eternal life. Behold, mine arm of mercy is extended towards you, and whosoever will come, him will I receive; and blessed are those who come unto me." (3 Nephi 9:14)

- "The scriptures speak of His arms being open, extended, stretched out, and encircling. They are described as mighty and holy, arms of mercy, arms of safety, arms of love, 'lengthened out all the day long.'"[5]

ACTING ON THE INVITATION TO RECEIVE

For what doth it profit a man if a gift is bestowed upon him, and he receive not the gift? Behold, he rejoices not in that which is given unto him, neither rejoices in him who is the giver of the gift. (Doctrine and Covenants 88:33)

It's all good and well to know that a spiritual gift is being offered and believe it would be good for us to accept it. It's another thing for perfectionistic folks to feel they "deserve" or are "worthy" of the gift and actually make themselves accessible to it. I have found myself more permeable to receiving from the Lord when I step away from the idea of deserving or not deserving and worthy or unworthy. "Deserving" is a worldly concept that is not relevant and not helpful. Toss that one away as best you can. Worthiness, while an important gospel principle, is also not relevant to receiving the Savior as your ally. He is not available to you only after you become worthy but from the moment you reach out to Him, signaling that you are willing to begin receiving the gift He is offering. Elder Marvin J. Ashton said in April 1989 general conference, "We need to remove *unworthy* from our vocabulary and replace it with *hope* and *work*"[6] (emphasis in original). More recently, Elder Dieter F. Uchtdorf said: "From the very moment we set foot upon the pathway of discipleship, seen and unseen blessings from God begin to attend us."[7]

So how might you send your personal signal that you want to receive your Savior? Some things that help me are singing, saying aloud scriptures as part of my prayers, and having art in my home that depicts the Savior.

Singing

Sing unto the Lord; for he hath done excellent things: this is known in all the earth. (Isaiah 12:5)

The Lord has told us that "the song of the righteous is a prayer unto me" (Doctrine and Covenants 25:12). If you don't feel you're one of "the righteous," then substitute something that feels right for you at the moment, such as "the seeker," "the willing," "the trying."

But, you say, "I can't sing!" What you mean is, "I can't sing well." Everyone can sing. It doesn't matter if you're off tune or raspy or think you sound silly. In my opinion, if you're perfectionistic, singing works *even better for this purpose* if you don't have musical ability. Being willing to sing despite lack of skill helps you step away from the perfection trap.

That willingness becomes a tender proffer of humility to your Savior. As you take this risk of trusting your Savior to "hear" you regardless of your lousy voice, you will find your heart softening and becoming more receptive to him.

I've found hymns that are essentially first-person prayers to be especially helpful. Sometime soon when you're alone in your car, I dare you to sing aloud even one line of "I Know that My Redeemer Lives" without feeling the Spirit rush in. It works. Other hymns that help me tell my Savior that I want to receive him into my life and my heart include:

Abide with Me 'Tis Eventide

Abide with me, 'tis eventide. The day is past and gone.

The shadows of the evening fall; The night is coming on.

Within my heart a welcome guest, Within my home abide.

Oh Savior, stay this night with me; Behold, 'tis eventide.

Oh Savior, stay this night with me; Behold, 'tis eventide.

Oh May My Soul Commune with Thee

Oh may my soul commune with thee

And find thy holy peace;

From worldly care and pain of fear,

Please bring me sweet release.

Nearer, My God, to Thee

Nearer, my God, to thee, nearer to thee.

E'en though it be a cross, that raiseth me.

Still all my song shall be, nearer, my God, to thee.

Nearer, my God, to thee, nearer to thee!

You might not have heard the last hymn below. If you haven't, listen to it on YouTube and become familiar with the simple tune. The words are an exquisite expression of the Savior's reaching out to each of us individually, waiting for us to receive Him.

Softly and Tenderly Jesus Is Calling

Softly and tenderly Jesus is calling.

Calling for you and for me.

Patiently Jesus is waiting and watching,

Watching for you and for me.

Come home, come home.

You who are weary, come home.

Earnestly, tenderly, Jesus is calling.

Calling, O sinner, come home!

Reciting Scriptures as Part of Personal Prayer

"And again, I command thee that thou shalt pray vocally as well as in thy heart; yea, before the world as well as in secret, in public as well as in private." (Doctrine and Covenants 19:28)

We can use the combined power of holy words plus our audible voice in our prayers to draw closer to Jesus Christ. We're often counseled to pray aloud at least some of the time for good reason. Doing so helps us stay on track, while silent prayer makes us more vulnerable to wandering thoughts. The audible sound of words carries a power that words in our minds alone lack.

Here are a few scriptures, spoken aloud during prayer, that help me become more receptive to my Savior. I've included after each verse one possible way to make the words first-person, giving them even more power as you pray. As you study the scriptures, keep an eye out for verses that might help you become more receptive to the Savior and adapt them for your prayers.

Come unto Christ . . . and partake of his salvation, and the power of his redemption. Yea, come unto him, and offer your whole souls as an offering unto him. (Omni 1:26)

I want to come unto Christ and partake of his salvation and the power of his redemption. Help me come unto Him. Help me offer my whole soul to Him.

O all ye that are pure in heart, lift up your heads and receive the pleasing word of God, and feast upon his love. (Jacob 3:2)

I want to have a purer heart. I want to receive the pleasing word of God. I want to feast upon his love. Please help me.

Behold, mine arm of mercy is extended towards you, and whosoever will come, him will I receive; and blessed are those who come unto me. (3 Nephi 9:14)

I believe that His mercy is extended toward me. I believe that He will receive me. Please bless me and help me as I strive to come unto Your Son.

Behold, he has brought them into his everlasting light, yea, into everlasting salvation; and they are encircled about with the matchless bounty of his love. (Alma 26:15)

Please bring me into your everlasting light and your everlasting salvation. Encircle me with the matchless bounty of your love.

Listen to the voice of Jesus Christ, your Redeemer, the Great I Am, whose arm of mercy hath atoned for your sins; Who will gather his people even as a hen gathereth her chickens under her wings, even as many as will hearken to my voice and humble themselves before me, and call upon me in mighty prayer. (Doctrine and Covenants 29:1–2)

Help me hear your voice, my dear Savior, who has atoned for my sins. Please let me gather as one of your people, even as a hen gathers her chickens under her wings. Help me hearken to your voice and humble myself before you. Help me as I keep learning how to call upon you in mighty prayer.

O have mercy, and apply the atoning blood of Christ that we may receive forgiveness of our sins, and our hearts may be purified; for we believe in Jesus Christ, the Son of God, who created heaven and earth, and all things; who shall come down among the children of men. (Mosiah 4:2)

O have mercy, and apply the atoning blood of Christ that I may receive forgiveness of my sins, and my heart may be purified; for I believe in Jesus Christ, the Son of God, who created heaven and earth, and all things; who shall come down among the children of men.

Drawing on the Power of Art That Depicts the Savior

You probably already have photos of temples, paintings of the Savior, and other religious art in your home. You might have chosen items that would appeal widely to all of your family members rather than those that speak to you personally. I would like to suggest that you select a few pieces just for you. They don't need to be costly—or cost anything at all.

For example, when I began to write this book, I printed and placed just to the left of my computer screen a public domain image of the Savior's face as depicted in Heinrich Hofmann's "Christ and the Rich Young Ruler." The copy is black-and-white and grainy. It speaks to me. It also reminds me that imperfect can be breathtaking.

A few suggestions for gathering your own images:

- Ask a child you love to draw or paint Jesus for you. Whatever he or she produces, it will have special meaning to you. Delight in its unpolished imperfection.

- Create art yourself that brings the Savior to your mind. No matter how rough or sketchy it turns out, value it for what it signifies to you.

- Print a variety of images from the Internet to broaden your perspective. Perfectionism can narrow and congeal our perspective. Let others' depictions of their love for Christ open up your heart.

As you build your collection and look often at the images, let them help you invite the Savior further into your heart and into your healing.

Notes

1. Larry Y. Wilson, "Only upon the Principles of Righteousness," *Ensign*, May 2012, 105.

2. David A. Bednar, "Seek Learning by Faith," *Ensign*, September 2007.

3. Gerald R. Lund, "Opening Our Hearts," *Ensign*, May 2008, 34.

4. Randall K. Bennett, "Choose Eternal Life," *Ensign*, November 2011, 100.

5. Neil L. Andersen, "Repent . . . that I May Heal You," *Ensign*, November 2009.

6.   Marvin J. Ashton, "On Being Worthy," *Ensign*, May 1989.

7.   Dieter F. Uchtdorf, "The Way of the Disciple," *Ensign,* May 2009, 76.

CHAPTER 10

Repenting without Getting Mired in Perfectionistic Hazards

The words *repent*, *repenting*, and *repentance* can raise anxiety for perfectionistic Latter-day Saints. If this chapter title is doing that for you, take a deep breath and keep an open mind. For me, anxiety around repentance began when I was a freshman at BYU. I took an honors religion course taught by one of the most revered professors on campus, and we delved deeply into gospel principles. I distinctly remember him telling us that when we repent, if we then repeat the sin we've repented of, our repentance is null and void—plus all our previously repented-of sins are heaped back upon us. Or at least that's what I thought I heard. It was a long time ago, and my perfectionistic filter was firmly in place. I'll never know in this lifetime exactly what he said.

I do know that the basis of this discussion was Doctrine and Covenants 82:7, where the Lord says to "go your ways and sin no more; but unto that soul who sinneth shall the former sins return, saith the Lord your God." My filter, unfortunately, prevented me from laying down in my memory the context of this verse. I know now that the Lord was speaking to "those among you who have sinned exceedingly." An *exceeding* sin, then, must not be repeated. If it is, then the way back is doubly hard. That might apply to many, and the principle does need to be accepted to return to the path toward eternal life. But most of you reading these pages are trying hard to do the right thing and don't face repenting of exceeding sin. Discussing repentance from serious sin is beyond my scope here but I will point out that President Spencer W. Kimball said, "sin has size and dimensions. There are greater and lesser ones."[1]

In my young perfectionistic mind, the context of Doctrine and Covenants 82 (if ever discussed) was forgotten and all that remained was that I must not sin after repenting. If I did, as I knew I would, then I would be in even bigger trouble than I already was. Who in her right mind would repent with that understanding? Repentance was something to be avoided, not embraced.

I was not fully conscious of these thought processes at the time and still work to modify them. It's sad to me now that for a season in my life, reception of gospel principles was distorted by perfectionistic thinking to the degree that I was not able to receive and use the invitation to repent. In the words of Elder D. Todd Christofferson, that invitation is a divine "expression of love" and repentance is the "key to happiness here and hereafter."[2] I believe those words with all my heart. To avoid repentance is to deprive ourselves of the full depth of joy that is being offered to us.

Perfectionists tend to think in terms of all-or-nothing.[3] ("If I can't reach my ideal weight, I'll give up on healthy eating altogether" or "If I can't find the perfect match, I won't marry anyone"). Like the experience I related above, some of us think we must repent with one giant *mea culpa* and then be perfect going forward. We know this doesn't work, but some of us try it over and over again anyway. Kindly nudging ourselves toward a more gentle, step-by-step approach will yield the gradual progress that is more realistic.

Elder David Bednar suggested this method in a general conference talk. Though he was not speaking of repentance specifically, the principle applies: "The Lord's pattern for spiritual development is 'line upon line, precept upon precept, here a little and there a little' (2 Nephi 28:30). *Small, steady, incremental spiritual improvements* are the steps the Lord would have us take" (emphasis added).[4]

REPENTING WITHOUT GETTING MIRED IN PERFECTIONISTIC HAZARDS

THE HAZARD OF FORGETTING THAT REPENTANCE IS AN ONGOING PROCESS

As I've searched the scriptures and the writings of Church leaders for words and principles about repentance that can be especially helpful to perfectionists, I've found a rich supply. They explain that repentance is not a one-time event but an ongoing process. We can't expect ourselves to eradicate all at once the pesky, errant, and entrenched negative habits we developed long ago. Elder D. Todd Christofferson said in October 2011 general conference that "real repentance, real change *may require repeated attempts*" (emphasis added).[5] I know by experience that my first try at repenting rarely "takes," so I am comforted by those words.

Elder Neil L. Anderson made similar comments during the October 2009 general conference:

> Sometimes in our repentance, in our daily efforts to become more Christlike, we find ourselves repeatedly struggling with the same difficulties. As if we were climbing a tree-covered mountain, at times we don't see our progress until we get closer to the top and look back from the high ridges. Don't be discouraged. If you are striving and working to repent, you are in the process of repenting.[6]

Seeing repentance as an ongoing process prevents discouragement and empowers us to keep trying. The perfectionistic single father of an alcoholic daughter described to me how he is learning to accept the ongoing process idea. He has not been able to change his angry reactions to his daughter's alcoholic episodes as much as he had hoped, but he is making progress. He is learning to be patient with himself and to keep working at it. Here is his account of this journey so far:

> My daughter Jenny [name and details changed] has been in and out of rehab multiple times, and each time she comes out I try to give her a clean start. I let her stay with me for a few days while she looks for a job and finds an apartment. About eight years ago, one day after being released from her fourth or fifth rehab stint, I went downstairs to her bedroom and found her passed out drunk. An empty bottle of vodka was on the floor at the foot of the bed. I yelled at her to wake up, which she did—groggily—and I lashed out at her at the top of my lungs about her ungratefulness, her weakness, and her unbelievable nerve. Then I picked up the bottle of vodka and threw it at her. It was plastic, thank goodness.

I left her room, shaking with anger. By the time I reached the top of the stairs, I was completely ashamed of myself. I couldn't believe I had actually thrown an object at my daughter, whom I love with all my heart. When she was sober again, I apologized. She didn't remember any of the incident, which was a tender mercy.

I began at that point to direct my prayers less at hoping for her to change and more at asking for help with my own anger and impatience. Since then, Jenny has cycled on and off the wagon many more times, and I've gradually learned to react to her relapses with more patience. I've had to repent repeatedly, but my angry reactions have become far less frequent and far less wounding toward her.

An "episode" had not occurred for a very long time when just last week I lost it again. It wasn't as bad as the incident eight years ago, but it might have been if we had not been in public. I had driven her to the grocery store, and as we shopped I noticed that she seemed "off." She wasn't exactly drunk, but she was altered, and I was disgusted. I kept my feelings to myself. I had many other stressors going on, including a recent cut in income, and I could feel my frustration rising.

When we got to the checkout counter, she had a full basket and I had a few items in my own cart. I finished checking out first and waited for her. As the cashier loaded her last item into a grocery bag, Jenny discovered she didn't have her state-issued food card with her. She turned to me with her "help me" look, and the old anger was triggered. I gave her looks that could kill, not caring who saw my contempt, and angrily slid my own credit card through the card reader. When we got out to the car, I came unglued. I couldn't believe she had done this to me again. Why didn't she check for the card before leaving for the store? Couldn't she remember my recent loss of income? What was she on? She shrank in her seat and said she was sorry.

It took me a few hours to gather my wits, apologize, and ask Jenny for her forgiveness yet again. She gave it freely. I then went to my Heavenly Father in prayer, expressed remorse, and asked for his forgiveness—yet again. I thought I might feel He was displeased with me, but instead He helped me to see that despite this relapse of my own, overall I had made a lot of progress. I rose from my knees feeling hopeful that I could continue to improve. As I've continued to think about this incident, I feel He wants me to know that my imperfectness is acceptable to Him as long as I keep trying and keep progressing.

REPENTING WITHOUT GETTING MIRED IN
PERFECTIONISTIC HAZARDS

The Hazard of Concern for Our Public Image

Another hazard to repentance for perfectionists is our tendency to worry excessively about what others think of us. It's hard for us to follow James's advice that we confess our faults to each other (James 5:16) and perhaps even harder to absorb the Savior's warning: "Woe unto you, when all men shall speak well of you!" (Luke 6:26).

If one of your deepest fears is that others will see you as flawed, you're less likely to engage the help from others that you need to truly repent. Elder Neal A. Maxwell taught that repentance is not necessarily or always a solitary, private endeavor. Rather, it can be a community effort if we will allow it to be. "Support from others is especially crucial now. Hence, we are directed to be part of a caring community in which we all 'lift up the hands which hang down, and strengthen the feeble knees' (Doctrine and Covenants 81:5)."In cases of serious sin especially—those that might include confession and public forsaking—we can benefit when we allow others to be part of our repentance process. Elder Maxwell continues: "Genuine support and love from others—not isolation—are needed to sustain this painful forsaking and turning!"[7]

The Hazard of Getting Stuck in
Rumination and Remorse

If our transgressions and our sins be upon us, and we pine away in them, how should we then live? (Ezekiel 33:10.)

As we repent, it's helpful for perfectionists to understand our tendency to ruminate on mistakes and sins. Reviewing our performance over and over again is so natural that it seems we must have been made that way. But we weren't. It's something we learned so long ago that it just feels that way. It can be unlearned.

Retired BYU psychology professor Kenneth L. Higbee provides an especially hopeful view as we try to deal with our past errors and sins. In an article many years ago in the *Ensign,* he said that "mistakes are not only an acceptable part of life, but they may even be beneficial. The intelligent use of our mistakes helps us learn and grow; past failures may be guideposts to future successes."[8]

What, exactly, does he mean by "intelligent use"? He means learning what we can and then moving on. It's the moving on part that so many have trouble with. Reflecting and feeling remorse are good things. Ruminating on and marinating in our failures are not. They can harm our spirits in three ways, says Higbee:

1. Our sorrows, regrets, and anxieties may become so great that they get out of hand and interfere with successful daily living. For example, we may hesitate to try new things, and doubt and indecision may prevent us from trying wholeheartedly when we do try something new.

2. Sorrows, regrets, and anxieties may become so threatening that we flee from reality in order to avoid them. Severe depression has caused some people to retreat into a fantasy world to escape the unpleasantness of their real world.

3. The person who cannot tolerate himself as fallible is not likely to remain on good terms with himself. If we make too much of our failures, we are likely to have low self-esteem.[9]

Human memory is a strange thing. The most significant events in our lives, including our biggest mistakes or sins, become lodged in the memory centers of our brains. It's interesting to me that the Lord says He won't remember our sins once we've repented of them, but He does not take our human memory of them away. There's a good reason for that. We're here in mortal life not only to be tested but also to learn through experience—both positive and negative. If we forget the episodes that taught us the most, which are generally our biggest mistakes, we can't allow the wisdom gleaned from each episode to build and mature our faith. It can be tricky to embrace the reality that remembering things we would rather forget has a purpose and at the same time avoid ruminating on them in a way that keeps us from moving forward.

Elder Dieter F. Uchtdorf says that it is in the interest of the adversary, not ours, to believe that remembering our sins means we haven't been forgiven: "Satan is a liar; he tries to blur our vision and lead us away from the path of repentance and forgiveness. God did not promise that we would not remember our sins. Remembering will help us avoid making the same mistakes again."[10]

If you have a tendency to ruminate, you're at higher risk for getting stuck in the remorse part of repentance. Having remorse is good. Staying in remorse isn't. Higbee continues:

REPENTING WITHOUT GETTING MIRED IN
PERFECTIONISTIC HAZARDS

The Lord does not require us to grovel in remorse as part of repentance. Excessive remorse can lead to a morbid sense of guilt and inferiority that can lead to a loss of self-respect and can drain a person of the moral energy necessary to complete the remaining steps of repentance. Repentance involves turning back to living God's commandments as well as feeling remorse for having broken his commandments. Let us not dwell on the latter at the expense of the former.[11]

The Hazard of Failing to Forgive Ourselves

As a hospice chaplain, my task is to assist people who are nearing the end of their lives to feel peace and acceptance as best they can. Dying well is a form of work, and we labor together to deal with unfinished business, forgive and ask for forgiveness, reconcile with estranged loved ones, and purposefully review the past to uncover threads of goodness and meaning in their lives.

One of the most heartbreaking scenarios I witness is people suffering spiritually because they don't feel good enough to meet their Maker. It's especially distressing to see Latter-day Saints not feel the peace about dying that, by all accounts of family members, they've earned the right to. They often use the phrase "not good enough" to describe how they're feeling. For some, no matter what reassurances they receive from family, bishop, friends, or chaplain, they cannot accept that they are true disciples and that after death they will continue the journey toward eternal life.

The Lord requires us to forgive all those who hurt us, but we sometimes forget that this requirement applies to us too. Perfectionists might have trouble forgiving themselves more than most because feeling worthy—good enough—is a weak spot for us. But we can learn to be as merciful toward ourselves as we are toward others.

I recommend Wendy Ulrich's thoughtful treatment of this subject in her books *Forgiving Ourselves*[12] and *Weakness Is Not Sin*.[13]

The Hazard of Believing the Atonement Is For
Everyone Else and Trying to Save Ourselves

Many of us have trouble believing that the Atonement applies to us. We've trained ourselves to be hyper-conscientious, strive until we drop, and do our utmost at every endeavor. When we read the scripture that we're saved by the grace of Jesus Christ "after all we can do" (2 Nephi

25:23), we know with certainty that we haven't yet done "all," so the Atonement cannot possibly apply. It applies to our saintly home teacher who is good and kind and giving all the time, but not to us. This disbelief can cause us years of unnecessary anguish and inappropriate guilt after we have repented. We may have faith that the Lord *can* forgive us, but we don't truly believe that he *will*. In a vicious cycle, that lack of belief can drain away our motivation to keep repenting—or even to repent in the first place.

How can this cycle be stopped?

We can begin by becoming conscious that it is not the Savior who has decided his Atonement doesn't apply to us, but rather it is we who have made that decision. When we can own up that we in fact have this fundamental belief about ourselves, even though we know it's irrational, we can begin to change our belief.

It helps to remember that our perfectionism is a weakness that is getting in the way of receiving our Savior. It is a human weakness, not a sin. (It might cause us to hurt ourselves and others at times, which can amount to sin, but the fact that we have this tendency is not a sin in itself.) The Atonement covers weaknesses as well as sin. That means that as we have faith in Christ—as we receive Him—He can help us overcome this weakness. His grace is not there only after all we can do, but it is also there *as* we work toward doing all we can.

Another help is to pin down why we believe we're not within the Atonement's reach. Maybe you feel unworthy so you don't qualify. Maybe you think the concept is too mysterious and nebulous and if you can't wrap your brain around it, how can you have faith in it? Carefully examine your own belief or disbelief. It might take a good amount of time to do this. Set aside that time. It is one of the most important insights you will ever seek.

For me, the insight came in a most unexpected way. I had been studying the Atonement in depth, trying to understand it better and wondering where I stood in "qualifying" for it. I read books like Spencer W. Kimball's *The Miracle of Forgiveness*, Tad McCallister's *The Infinite Atonement*, Stephen Robinson's *Believing Christ*, and James Ferrell's *The Peacegiver*. I scrutinized sermons about the Atonement in the Book of Mormon, even copying and pasting them into one long document with the intention of examining them again in one big gulp. I reviewed masterful sermons about the Atonement from Church leaders, such as Bruce Hafen's "The Atonement: All for All." He talks about the high price of qualifying for "such exquisite treasure" as the Savior's grace and that "we must give the way Christ gave—every drop He had." His closing paragraph says, "May we not shrink when we discover, paradoxically, how dear a price we must pay to receive what is, finally, a gift from Him. When the Savior's all and our all come together, we will find not only forgiveness of sin, 'we shall see him as he is,' and 'we shall be *like him*.'"[14]

Had I paid that "dear price" yet? Had I given "every drop"? How would I know?

I drank deeply from President Marion G. Romney's First Presidency Message in the December 1973 *Ensign*, titled "Christ's Atonement: The Gift Supreme." This passage struck me in particular:

> It is the aspect of the Atonement that will raise men "unto life eternal" that we are considering here. It is not necessary to await the resurrection to receive the blessing of this aspect of the resurrection. Amulek, teaching the Nephites, said: "[N]ow is the time and the day of your salvation; and therefore, if ye will repent, and harden not your hearts, *immediately* shall the great plan of redemption be brought about unto you" (Alma 34:31).
>
> When a person qualifies himself to receive the blessing of this aspect of Christ's Atonement, he is by the power of God forgiven of his sins; he is born again of the Spirit; he is a new person; he takes on the divine nature; he has "no more disposition to do evil, but to do good continually" (Mosiah 5:2); he has peace of conscience and is filled with joy. (See Mosiah 4:3; emphasis in original).[14]

Had I qualified myself to receive these blessings? I knew I had at least some disposition still to do evil. Did that disqualify me? I had some peace but not all that much. I was filled with joy on occasion but not often. Did that mean I had not yet qualified?

I also read Elder M. Russell Ballard's "The Atonement and the Value of One Soul," including this statement about qualifying to access the Atonement:

> The gift of resurrection and immortality is given freely through the loving grace of Jesus Christ to all people of all ages, regardless of their good or evil acts. And to those who choose to love the Lord and who show their love and faith in Him by keeping His commandments and qualifying for the full blessings of the Atonement, He offers the additional promise of exaltation and eternal life, which is the blessing of living in the presence of God and His Beloved Son forever.[15]

Did I love the Lord enough? Had I kept the commandments well enough to qualify for the full blessings of the Atonement?

As I continued to study and search and talk with others about their understanding of the Atonement—all of this in a fairly compressed period of a few months—someone led me to a statement by Elder Bruce R. McConkie. I don't remember who it was, but I do remember that when I read it, I found a measure of relief from my anxieties. Speaking to the Salt Lake Institute of Religion in 1982, he said:

> Everyone in the Church who is on the straight and narrow path, who is striving and struggling and desiring to do what is right, though far from perfect in this life; if he passes out of this life while he's on the straight and narrow, he's going to go on to eternal reward in his Father's kingdom.
>
> We don't need to get a complex or get a feeling that you have to be perfect to be saved. . . . The way it operates is this: you get on the path that's named the "straight and narrow." You do it by entering the gate of repentance and baptism. The straight and narrow path leads from the gate of repentance and baptism, a very great distance, to a reward that's called eternal life. . . . Now is the time and the day of your salvation, so if you're working zealously in this life—though you haven't fully overcome the world and you haven't done all you hoped you might do—you're still going to be saved.[16]

It seemed to me that I was on the path Elder McConkie described, and it felt good to think that I was. But I wasn't sure. Was I working "zealously"? That is a high standard. Was I meeting it?

I didn't know.

I kept thinking and pondering and wondering, unsettled by the prospect that if I didn't qualify, I didn't know what more I could do. I was at my limit of feeling inadequate and anxious about this. I had to push the thoughts and feelings away and just live my life. Which I did.

At some point later—perhaps a few days or maybe a few weeks—I was doing one of my usual mundane household chores. I opened the door leading out of my kitchen into my garage, my thoughts centered around finding a tool. As I stepped onto the threshold, the following words came unbidden to my mind:

"You are on the path."

They were not my words nor my thoughts. They were nowhere near the Atonement and whether I qualified for it. My mind had been on my task.

I immediately knew the implication—the Atonement applied to me. I qualified—right here and right now in a mundane place while doing a mundane task. Not in some distant future after I had zealously done more, and not while I was serving in the temple or singing in Church or magnifying my calling.

What I had to do was stay on the path of discipleship, no matter how steep the climb. If I did, my exaltation was assured.

Relief and release slowly came over me. They were not overwhelming feelings but subtle and restrained. Over time, I realized that my anxieties were abating and peace was building. The peace too was understated—almost delicate. It increased slowly and steadily as the implications of the Lord's words to me unfolded further, sank in, and became part of my life.

I have never returned to my former level of anxiety about whether I qualify for the Atonement. I have my moments, but the gift of peace from that day has been with me to greater and lesser degrees ever since. As I look back, I did not think at the time that I had done everything in my power to merit such a sublime moment of grace. (A number of years later, I still have that document of Book of Mormon Atonement sermons on my computer, and every once in awhile I think about finding time to study it, but I haven't.) I discovered that the Lord's definition of "after all I can do" is different from mine. It is far more generous and merciful than I thought possible.

As you seek your own reassurance about your standing before the Lord, be diligent but not overzealous. Work at it, then give it a rest. We can't orchestrate when or how the Lord will grant His tender mercies, but He will. I know that He will.

Notes

1. Spencer W. Kimball, "What Is True Repentance?" *New Era*, May 1974.

2. Todd D. Christofferson, "The Divine Gift of Repentance," *Ensign*, November 2011.

2. For further information about all-or-nothing thinking, see *When Perfect Isn't Good Enough*, by Martin M. Antony and Richard P. Swinson (Oakland, CA: New Harbinger Publications, 2009), 48–50.

3. David A. Bednar, "Clean Hands and a Pure Heart," *Ensign*, October 2007, 82.

4. Christofferson, "The Divine Gift of Repentance," 39.

5. Neil L. Andersen, "Repent . . . that I May Heal You," *Ensign*, November 2009.

6. Neal A. Maxwell, "Repentance," *Ensign*, November 1991.

7. Kenneth L. Higbee, "Forgetting Those Things Which Are Behind," *Ensign*, September 1972.

8. Ibid.

9. Dieter F. Uchtdorf, "Point of Safe Return," *Ensign*, May 2007.

10. Higbee, "Forgetting Those Things Which Are Behind."

11. Wendy Ulrich, *Forgiving Ourselves: Getting Back Up When We Let Ourselves Down* (Salt Lake City: Deseret Book, 2008).

12. Wendy Ulrich, *Weakness Is Not Sin: The Liberating Distinction That Awakens Our Strengths* (Salt Lake City: Deseret Book, 2009).

13. Marion G. Romney, "Christ's Atonement: The Gift Supreme," *Ensign*, December 1973.

14. Bruce C. Hafen, "The Atonement: All for All," *Ensign*, May 2004.

15. M. Russell Ballard, "The Atonement and the Value of One Soul," *Ensign*, May 2004.

16. Bruce R. McConkie, "The Probationary Test of Mortality," Salt Lake Institute of Religion devotional, 10 January 1982, 12.

CHAPTER 11

Handling Anxiety-Provoking Scriptures

$\mathcal{I}$ want to speak candidly about several scriptures that can trip up perfectionistic Latter-day Saints if we don't take into account our personal vulnerability. My discussion risks coming across as minimizing or downplaying the importance of scriptural passages that are key to understanding the Atonement and our personal salvation. I want to be clear that I am *not* playing down their importance but rather am exploring their meaning in a way I hope will be helpful to perfectionist Latter-day Saints. I know from personal experience that the perfectionistic mind-set can filter words—even sacred words—in a way that creates distance from our Savior. As a recovering perfectionist, I deeply desire to help others like me to see these scriptures in a way that brings them closer to Christ.

"BE YE THEREFORE PERFECT"

First, let's take a look at the Savior's teaching to "Be ye therefore perfect, even as your Father which is in heaven is perfect" (Matthew 5:48). He conveys the same imperative in the Book of Mormon this way: "I would that ye should be perfect even as I, or your Father who is in heaven

103

is perfect" (3 Nephi 12:48). Notice that He doesn't refer to Himself as perfect in the Matthew version but does so in the Book of Mormon verses after His death and resurrection. Even He did not attain perfection until after mortality.

We've already reviewed many statements from Church leaders that perfection cannot be achieved in this life, but it's also important to understand the rich meanings that can be drawn from the original Greek word *teleios*, that is translated as "perfect" in Matthew 5:48. Most of us have heard or read that *teleios* doesn't mean perfect in the English sense of the word but rather has several different possible meanings. The most common connotations spoken of among Latter-day Saints are "finished," "complete" and "whole." But according to LDS scholar John W. Welch, the Savior might have intended much broader and richer meanings. For example, He says, "This word is used in Greek religious literature to describe the person who has become fully initiated in the rituals of a religion." It can also mean "perfect or 'undivided in obedience to God' and 'unlimited love'" and "advancement from one level to a next level, going on to become 'perfect,' 'finished,' or 'completed' in an individual's instruction and endowment."[1] Welch discusses even further possible meanings that you can explore if you're interested.

Elder Russell M. Nelson taught that the meaning is not "without an error" but rather "implies 'achieving a distant objective.'"[2] He quotes scholar David Hill, who says that "the emphasis is not on flawless moral character, but on whole-hearted devotion to the imitation of God—not in the perfection of his being, but of his ways."[3]

Perhaps Brigham Young, with his no-nonsense, pragmatic style, gave us the best strategy for reducing perfectionistic anxiety this scripture might raise for some of us: "If the . . . passage is not worded to our understanding, we can alter the phraseology . . . , and say, "Be ye as perfect as ye can."[4] For the most thorough discussion I know of possible meanings of the word *perfect* in both the Old Testament and New Testament, take a look at a talk from the 2010 BYU Sperry Symposium given by Frank F. Judd Jr., an associate professor of ancient scripture at BYU.[5]

"After All We Can Do"

In 2 Nephi 25, written by Nephi's brother Jacob, Nephi is preaching to the people of Nephi. They see him as "a king or a protector," and he tells them that he is laboring diligently to write the prophecies of others and of himself for this reason: "To persuade our children, and also our brethren, to believe in Christ, and to be reconciled to God; for we know that it is by grace that we are saved, after all we can do" (2 Nephi 25:23).

Let's take a closer look at the phrase "after all we can do." I confess that it has in the past raised my perfectionistic anxiety and sometimes still does—though much less so since I felt a deep reassurance about this as I related in chapter 9.

How can we possibly ever say we've done "all" we can? Anytime I think about my behavior yesterday or today, I can see something more I could have done to be right before God. There's always room for improvement. If I had done *all* I could on any particular day, wouldn't that mean I had behaved perfectly? My perfectionistic brain sometimes leads me to understand "all we can do" as "already perfect." Perfectionists, after all, believe in the possibility of perfection, so if true all-out effort is expended, surely that would equal perfect.

That's poor reasoning, of course, and an example of how perfectionism can distort our thinking. It's comforting to me to remember President Spencer W. Kimball's words that "each of us has more opportunities to do good and to be good than we ever use."[6] His subtext seems to be that it is *not* possible to do our "all" *all* of the time.

Even phrases like "do your best" or "give your best effort," which might work well for non-perfectionists, can raise anxiety and desperate feelings to measure up. When perfectionists hear that all the Lord expects of us is "our best," we hear: "Give your maximum effort 100 percent of the time." We know that's not possible, but some of us aim for it anyway. It's part of the perfectionism con that after a performance, no matter how good, we believe we could have done better. Personally, when I hear "best" phrases, I adjust them in my mind so that the message is manageable. For example, if someone in a church setting says that what's expected of me is not perfection but only my best, I'll say to myself, "What's expected of me is diligence."

Some of the anxiety about the phrase "all we can do" comes from a misunderstanding about timing. Nephi is speaking of the final judgment when our mortal lives are over. If we don't keep that in mind, we might believe that we're a candidate for Christ's grace only after we've done all we can. Elder Bruce C. Hafen corrects this idea in his book *The Broken Heart.* "The Savior's gift of grace to us is not necessarily limited in time to 'after' all we can do. We may receive his grace before, during, and after the time when we expend our own efforts."[7]

In my study for this book, I found a phrase that brought me peace when I read it rather than feelings of discouragement. The words were written by Elder D. Todd Christofferson in an *Ensign* article. Here is what he said:

> Personal persistence in the path of obedience is something different than achieving perfection in mortality. Perfection is not, as some suppose, a prerequisite for justification and sanctification. It is just the opposite: justification (being pardoned) and sanctification (being purified) are the prerequisites for perfection. We only become perfect "in Christ" (see Moroni 10:32), not independently of Him. Thus, what is required of us in order to obtain mercy in the day of judgment is *simple diligence*" (emphasis added).[8]

Similarly, Elder Dieter F. Uchtdorf said in October 2010 general conference: "*Diligently* doing the things that matter most will lead us to the Savior of the world."[9]

He didn't say "frantically" or "speedily" or "hastily" doing the things that matter most. Just "diligently."

Since I noticed that word, I have heard it and read it from our leaders often. Very often.

"Simple diligence" is now my mantra whenever I think I am not doing enough or being good enough. It is a gentle reminder to slowly and surely, with "small, steady, incremental"[10] steps, become the person I hope my Savior will greet someday with open arms.

"The Great Plan of Happiness"

At dinner with friends recently, we got to talking about how Church leaders seem to be emphasizing the gospel's "plan of happiness" more and more. Some wondered about the word *happiness*, which can be viewed as a fleeting emotion. Words like *joy* and *peace* suggest a deeper, more enduring feeling, they argued.

One person offered, "Well, it's not like 'the plan of happiness' phrase is scripture." "Oh, yes it is!" said another.

In fact, the phrase occurs twice in the Book of Mormon:

> "*Now behold, it was not expedient that man should be reclaimed from this temporal death, for that would destroy the great plan of happiness*" (*Alma 42:8*).

and

"Now, repentance could not come unto men except there were a punishment, which also was eternal as the life of the soul should be, affixed opposite to the plan of happiness, which was as eternal also as the life of the soul" (Alma 42:16).

Both times it is spoken by Alma the Younger in his masterful sermon to his audience of one: his son Corianton. Alma uses the phrase as a synonym for the plan of salvation. He works hard to persuade his son that this plan will lead him to eternal life—which is eternal happiness. As he describes this plan, it is clear that encompassed within the word *happiness* are all the attributes of eternal life, including peace and joy. As Mosiah said, eternal life is "a state of never-ending happiness" (Mosiah 4:41).

Several years ago, when I first noticed "the plan of happiness" being mentioned more by Church leaders, I was dismayed by a few statements that Latter-day Saints should be the happiest people in the world because of their knowledge of this plan. "So," I thought, "I'm supposed to read my scriptures every day, pray several times a day, do family history work, attend the temple often, magnify my callings, pay my tithing, attend all my church meetings, keep a journal, plant a garden, read the *Ensign*, develop my talents, repent continually, do my visiting teaching—AND BE HAPPY! Seriously? I'm *supposed* to be happy too?" As a recovering perfectionist, I did not welcome one more "should." I wanted my happiness to unfold naturally from living the gospel, not be another item on "The List." This was the anxious, raw-nerve-ending reaction of a perfectionist. It was harder at the time for me to perceive the loving invitation to happiness being offered by Heavenly Father and by those quoting the scriptures.

My personal adjustment is simply to set aside the "should" part and focus on the "happiness" part. My Heavenly Father has given me His plan because He wants happiness, peace, and joy for me. With the extra pressures I already tend to feel because of perfectionistic tendencies, He doesn't want the "Great Plan of Happiness" to be yet another pressure but rather *an invitation*.

NEGOTIATING YOUR PERSONAL FILTER

With the three scriptural passages we've discussed as examples, I would like to propose a technique for managing occasions when you come across a scripture or statement from a Church leader that stirs up your perfectionism. You know the feeling. Your heart sinks a little, your gut tightens, your stomach feels vaguely sick. Your anxiety rises, your mood drops, and your desire to continue reading evaporates. These signals can be confusing because you believe that the words are sacred and true, but your feelings that accompany the words are negative. When these feelings arise, the following technique can help:

• Acknowledge your feelings honestly and fully. They're real, so don't try to pretend you don't have them. Pretending, even if only to yourself, keeps you from the truth, which constrains you in your perfectionism rather than frees you from it.

• Pray for help as you work to disentangle your negative feelings from the words you're reading or hearing.

• Embrace the principle that our feelings are not necessarily an accurate reflection of reality. Feelings are not facts. Be open to that possibility.

• Read the full context of the scripture or teaching to get as accurate an understanding as possible for what the writer or speaker is trying to communicate. Study the context. Scrutinize for subtext. Read any footnotes and cross-references.

• Tinker with alternate wording or additional wording that feels right for you given your personal filter. Check in with the Lord about whether your adjustments are pleasing to Him. (Consider the possibility that you're rationalizing—but don't get stuck there.) For example, when I read or hear the scripture "after all we can do," I adjust it slightly so that it reads, "after all I can diligently do in this life."

• For the scriptures or words from Church leaders that trigger your negative feelings most, use this technique over time and keep making further adjustments. This is *your personal salvation* that you're working out with the Lord. He wants to be your partner, and He'll help you if you'll let Him. You would not be the first to have your personal wrestle with the Lord over your salvation.

NOTES

1.   John W. Welch, "New Testament Word Studies," *Ensign*, April 1993.

2.   Russell M. Nelson, "Perfection Pending," *Ensign*, November 1995.

3.   David Hill, *The Gospel of Matthew* (Grand Rapids, MI: Eerdmans, 1972), 131.

4.   Brigham Young, *Discourses of Brigham Young*, J.A. Widtsoe, Ed. (Salt Lake City: Deseret Book, 1954), 89.

5.   Frank F. Judd, Jr., "'Be Ye Therefore Perfect: The Elusive Quest for Perfection," Sperry Symposium, www.byu.edu.

6.   Spencer W. Kimball, "Jesus: The Perfect Leader," *Ensign*, August 1979.

7.   Bruce C. Hafen, *The Broken Heart: Applying the Atonement to Life's Experiences* (Salt Lake City: Deseret Book, 1989), 155.

8.   D. Todd Christofferson, "Justification and Sanctification," *Ensign*, June 2001.

9.   Dieter F. Uchtdorf, "Of Things that Matter Most," *Ensign*, November 2011, 21.

10.   David A. Bednar, "Clean Hands and a Pure Heart," *Ensign*, November 2007.

.

CHAPTER 12

Praying and Feeling the Spirit

Will ye not now return unto me . . . that I may heal you? . . . If ye will come unto me ye shall have eternal life. Behold, mine arm of mercy is extended towards you, and whosoever will come, him will I receive. (3 Nephi 9:13–14)

For us perfectionistic folks, asking for help from anyone is a dicey proposition. We don't like to be exposed as needing help, even to our Heavenly Father. Asking for help blows our cover. At the same time, we tend to feel inside a deep inadequacy and unworthiness, no matter how hard we've tried to behave adequately and worthily. It's hard for us to pray when we feel unworthy, which turns out to be most of the time. Elder J. Devn Cornish recognized this tendency in so many of us: "There is a risk that a person may not feel good enough to pray. . . . It is as tragic to think we are too sinful to pray as it is for a very sick person to believe he is too sick to go to the doctor!"[1]

There is no "worthy" or "unworthy" when it comes to praying. If we're willing to ask, our Heavenly Father wants to answer. We might have more or less difficulty *discerning answers* to our prayers depending on the sensitivity of our spiritual receptors.

Part of the difficulty for some is that they turn off all feelings. Feelings can be confusing and make us feel out of control, especially when they swing to extremes. To prevent fluctuations, some turn it all off. They don't realize that their self-anesthetizing negates the possibility of joy as well as sorrow. The Spirit communicates largely through our feelings, as President Ezra Taft Benson said: "We hear the words of the Lord most often by a feeling. If we are humble and sensitive, the Lord will prompt us through our feelings."[2]

If we're humble, we might become very frustrated when we're unable to discern the Spirit, not realizing that we also need *sensitivity*. Sensitivity requires being open to feelings. For those who numb their feelings, it's not that the Lord has stopped trying to speak to you; it's that you've unwittingly turned off the very receptors that would allow you to have the spiritual feelings you long for. You have indeed heard his voice, as Nephi said, but "ye were past feeling, that ye could not *feel* his words" (1 Nephi 17:45, emphasis added). You don't have to be wicked or evil to be past feeling. Maybe you just hurt too much for too long and had to get some relief by going numb. We all use numbing sometimes, but if you're zoning out on the Internet for hours at a time, watching too much TV, and taking hobbies to an extreme, you might be numbing addictively. If so, consider counseling to help you restore your feelings.

Perfectionists also typically have such a strong inner critic who chatters inside their heads constantly that it's difficult to hear the gentle, soft, and loving voice of the Spirit. We're listening for a voice like ours—or like the critical parent we might have had—and the Lord doesn't speak that way to His children.

Though I'm no longer a "practicing perfectionist" but rather a recovering one, I continue to struggle with discerning the Spirit in my life. I've experienced sublime moments of feeling the Spirit, but they remain few and far between. It took me a long time to realize that my difficulties in this arena are not because I'm spiritually defective or spiritually tone-deaf. Mostly I'm just anxious. It's difficult to feel the Spirit when we're anxious. That reality has seemed so unfair to me at times because we anxious folks need the calming power of the Spirit more than most!

But the truth is that anxiety is a form of internal speed, and speed is generally not conducive to the Spirit of the Lord. When we're anxious, our heart beats faster, our thoughts spin, our gut whirls. In contrast, the Spirit is slow, subtle, and quiet. Perfectionism is both a source of anxiety and an accelerator for anxiety once it gets started. I had a tough experience with this principle when I was fifteen, though I was too young and unaware to learn from it at the time. I decided to enter a Utah state piano competition. I chose a dazzling contemporary piece that required blinding finger speed that I felt sure would get the judge's attention. I remember the piece well even these forty years later—"Der Jongleur" ("The Juggler") by Ernst Toch. During the first round of competition, I was scared stiff but performed well. I received the maximum score from all the judges and was advanced to the state level.

Piano competitions are brutal. They're also fertile ground for planting or growing perfectionism. It is absolutely unacceptable to use music, so you must memorize every note completely and perfectly. Every missed or incorrect note counts against you, so your fingers must behave flawlessly as well. I had an outstanding memory as a youth. At age twelve, still fearless and self-confident, a friend and I had performed without music and without a hitch a glittery two-piano piece for the seventy-fifth anniversary celebration of our small New Jersey borough. But by fifteen, by then living in Utah, I had developed the self-consciousness and anxiety of adolescence. Anxiety interferes with the memory retrieval process in the brain, and it was interfering with my piano performances. I had already frozen during piano recitals, resulting in complete immobilization of my fingers. These performances were not only imperfect—they were disasters as far I was concerned. It was humiliating to be forced to stop playing, think hard, and begin playing again. I had learned to double and triple memorize a few pick-up spots in every piece just in case.

The day of the Utah state competition, I was terrified. As I rode a school bus to Salt Lake City along with my fellow Provo High musicians, my stomach churned and my head pounded. Waiting for my turn to perform was almost unbearable. When the moment finally arrived, my fingers shook as I handed a copy of my music to each of the four judges. I adjusted the piano bench, tried to calm myself, and began to play. I made it through the first page before I froze. The notes fled from my memory. I stopped momentarily, scanning my brain for one of the pick-up spots I had memorized. The only one I could recall was the first few measures of the last page. As I resumed playing, in my peripheral vision I could see the judges flipping through the pages of music, trying to figure out where I was. A three-minute piece turned into a thirty-second piece.

When it was over, I got up and studiously avoided eye contact as I walked past the judges. As my pre-performance anxiety abated, my post-performance anxiety exploded. I had failed miserably, and I was mortified.

I never competed again.

To this day, I am happy to play the piano for anyone at any time—as long as I can use my "cheat sheet"—the printed music. That works well for keeping my anxiety around musical performance at bay. I enjoy playing for others now and even performing from time to time.

So how is this experience related to our anxiety around prayer "performance"? Or anxieties around difficulty feeling the Spirit given our tendency to think we're not up to that ultimate prerequisite for inspiration from the Lord—worthiness? For many Latter-day Saints, all the verbal reassurance in the world that we're worthy and that we too can feel the Spirit are not likely to get through.

Why should this be so? It doesn't seem fair that a form of suffering—anxiety and its close cousin, depression—should keep the Spirit away. I have felt angry about this on occasions when I've desperately wanted answers to questions posed in prayer but not felt they came or at times I hoped just to feel that comforting warm blanket around me that people talk about but didn't. "Lord, why can't you just punch through my mortal weaknesses and *talk to me*? Shouldn't your Spirit be able to penetrate this 'stuff' of mine that I'm working on but is still in the way?" I don't know any definitive answers to those questions, but I have some ideas about why anxiety seems to be a block to feeling the Spirit and discerning answers to our prayers.

First, anxiety is connected to our agency. It is not exclusively an agency matter, as some of us are born with more of a tendency toward anxiety than others. But as adults, anxiety is to a large degree within our control. When the "what-ifs" enter our minds—"What if I don't get an answer?", "What if it's wrong for me to even ask this?", "What if I don't like the answer?", "What if I'm not worthy enough to merit an answer?"—then our heads and hearts fill with fear. As we learn to stop the what-iffing, we can quiet our fears and let the Spirit enter. It is a matter of using our agency to decrease our fears and replace them with faith as best we can.

A second aspect of anxiety around prayer is our desire to control the outcome. In general, perfectionists are controlling. We believe that if we can control what happens to us, we can relieve our anxiety. This belief gets in the way of personal revelation because it transfers trust in the Lord to trust in ourselves. Even the mere prospect of trusting the Lord—and allowing all the unknowns that accompany that trust—can trigger our anxious what-iffing. "What if I trust him but he lets me down?" We might manage to trust him for a while, but if our anxiety rises high enough, it becomes intolerable and we revert to trusting ourselves instead and then try to control the outcome.

Our agency is absolutely sacred to our Heavenly Father, and he will not impinge on it. He wants us to work out our anxieties, fears, and neurotic needs.

So—we perfectionistic folks need some extra help to moderate our anxieties so we can feel the Spirit. How can we "use our music" to feel less anxious when we try to pray and listen for the still, small voice? I suggest that a "cheat sheet" works for this too. Because we're dealing with sacred matters, though, let's call it something more befitting. Let's call it a "Spirit Prompt." (If that phrase doesn't work for you, choose one that does.)

Spirit Prompt One—Slow the Spin.

I didn't know how to slow the spin as a teenaged would-be concert pianist. I probably could have gotten some help for it if I had verbalized my feelings to anyone, but I didn't. Later I was able to verbalize my anxieties around feeling the Spirit to several trusted people, and with their help I have been able to moderate my anxieties over time, though they're still a challenge. Here are suggestions for praying:

- Sit still and don't say anything for awhile. Just be still.

- Ask the Lord to help you relax and quiet your mind.

- Express gratitude until your anxieties subside.

- After praying and saying "amen," spend at least a few more moments in silence.

- Don't expect a particular answer or a particular feeling.

- Be open to the possibility that an answer or feeling will come later, sometimes much later.

Spirit Prompt Two—Sing a Sacred Song.

For me, this is probably *the* most powerful way of dispelling anxiety and inviting the Spirit. I recently began not just singing to feel close to

God but singing the words of my prayers on occasion. This might sound strange, but it has a remarkable calming and soothing effect. All I do is make up a tune for the words I want to say to my Heavenly Father. Sometimes the tune gets repetitive. It doesn't matter.

The idea came from a rabbi friend and colleague, who often sings both private and public prayers. He once sang a prayer at my request, and the experience moved me to tears. If you're feeling stuck in your prayers, it's worth a try to sing them.

Spirit Prompt Three—Recite Scriptures Aloud.

As we discussed in Chapter 9, reciting scriptures aloud can be powerful. The opposite feeling to anxiety is peace, so consider choosing scriptures that impart peace. Here are a few you might recite—with adjustments to wording as you see fit to integrate them into your personal prayers.

> Peace I leave with you, my peace I give unto you: not as the world giveth, give I unto you. Let not your heart be troubled, neither let it be afraid. (John 14:27)

> Great peace have they which love thy law: and nothing shall offend them. (Psalm 119:165)

> Live in peace, and the God of love and peace shall be with you. (2 Corinthians 13:11)

> How beautiful upon the mountains are the feet of him that bringeth good tidings, that is the founder of peace, yea, even the Lord, who has redeemed his people; yea, him who has granted salvation unto his people. (Mosiah 15:18)

> But learn that he who doeth the works of righteousness shall receive his reward, even peace in this world, and eternal life in the world to come. (Doctrine and Covenants 59:23)

Adjusting Expectations About Testimony, Change of Heart, and Everyday Inspiration

With such high aspirations for themselves, many perfectionists have unrealistic expectations of just about everything, including spiritual experiences. I believe a perfectionistic filter causes us to "see" the more ideal version of things and reflexively aim for it without much thought. For example, as I was growing up, I "chose" to focus on my father's way of receiving personal revelation and filtered out my mother's. I didn't know I was doing this, of course. My mother didn't talk much about her spiritual experiences because, I later learned, they were of the quiet, small, steady variety. My father, on the other hand, spoke of visionary dreams, experiences with loved ones beyond the veil, and feeling the Spirit like "an electrical shock or current." I expected that I too would be blessed with striking spiritual experiences.

My first disappointment in this arena came at the age of eight when I was baptized. I was a serious child with a strong desire to do what was right, and I prepared with great soberness. When the day came, I was convinced that after being washed clean in the baptismal font, I could and would never sin again. As I came up out of the baptismal waters, I expected to feel a cleansing power well beyond the water literally washing over me. I didn't. I didn't know what to make of that. The next day was Fast Sunday and my confirmation. Again, I expected to feel something powerful and dramatic when my father laid his hands on my head and pronounced the words "receive the Holy Ghost." I felt nothing.

I was deeply disappointed. I didn't discuss my feelings with anyone and thus there was no opportunity for an adult to help me normalize my experience and reassure me that I wasn't spiritually defective (or for someone to tell me I had not sinned before my baptism because I was a not of accountable age, and thus there were no sins to wash away). I assumed I wasn't good enough and I would just have to try harder to be "worthy."

As the years went by and I still did not experience spiritually what I hoped for, I began to doubt. I felt my lack of a defining testimony experience meant I didn't have a "real" testimony. I began talking about my dilemma to others, who would try to reassure me. But my expectation was fixed. I could not let go of it. In my late thirties, as my angst grew over this disappointment, as well as others, I withdrew from church activity. Attending meetings felt to me like I was pretending that I knew what everyone else there apparently knew. I couldn't bear to be open in a Church setting about my doubts, disappointments, and fears. The perfectionist in me could not tolerate feeling like *or being seen as* one of those people who doesn't really "get it."

My journey to recognize my personal style of testimony was long and has many layers, but here is the relevant point for our discussion: Over time I came to understand that my testimony was a different variety than the "defining moment" type. Mine is what I now call a "process testimony." Sometimes I also call it a "cumulative testimony." Since reaching a large measure of peace about this, I've heard many others speak of their testimony in similar ways. A "process testimony" might even be the norm. Who would have thought?

Maybe people have become more open about the subtler styles of testimony or maybe my diminished perfectionistic filter enables me to give full weight to what I once considered an inferior testimony. I don't know. I do know that now, whenever I hear someone talk about not having a defining testimony moment, my antennae go up. I enjoy it when others validate my personal reality. For example, during general conference in October 2008, my ears perked up when Elder Carlos A. Godoy talked about his own testimony as a process and not a single defining moment. He recalled visiting a Sunday School class while traveling in Brazil:

> At some point in the lesson, the teacher asked the class members if they would share a powerful spiritual experience they had while developing their testimony of the Church. While some brothers and sisters were sharing their stories, I mentally reviewed my own experiences as a convert for something I could share with them, but I could not think of anything very remarkable in my process of gaining a testimony.
>
> While I was thinking and listening to the others' experiences, I realized that the teacher expected me to participate. She was listening to the other members, and she let me know that she was waiting for my great experience to be shared. After all, I was an Area Seventy, and I should have something impressive to share. Feeling that the time was passing and she was waiting for me, I tried harder to find something that would fit in this category of a powerful event, but I was not able to think of anything, to the disappointment of the teacher. For all I wanted to help, I could not meet her expectation.[3]

My eyes were riveted on him and my ears intent. I was so grateful to him for voicing as a General Authority what I had been feeling for so long. He then drew this lesson for all of us:

> A testimony then, for some people, may come through a single and irrefutable event. But for others, it may come through a process of experiences that, perhaps not as remarkable but when combined, testify in an indisputable way that what we have learned and lived is true.[4]

I encountered a similar account of testimony when I read on the Church's news media website the full transcript of Elder Dallin H. Oaks's interview with a filmmaker Helen Whitney. She created the PBS documentary *The Mormons*, and she asked Elder Oaks how his faith developed. He answered:

> Whether a person or how a person gets over the road in the development of their faith is suited to their own unique circumstances. I know for some the mountain of their faith originated in a volcanic eruption. The hot lava suddenly flowed, and then the mountain was constructed. For other people, it's a sedimentary deposit—a little bit at a time over time, trying this, trying that, learning this and learning that, challenging this and challenging that. And then one day it has accumulated a mountain. That's my experience, so I don't have a specific defining moment.[5]

Here was another confirmation that my more subtle way of knowing was on equal footing with the dramatic ways. I added the word "sedimentary" to my vocabulary for describing my testimony. I think this point bears repeating, so here are several more quotes from General Authorities: Speaking to the Young Women, Elder Henry B. Eyring said:

> Testimony will come to you in pieces as parts of the whole truth of the gospel of Jesus Christ are confirmed. . . . The answer [regarding the Book of Mormon] may not come in a single and powerful spiritual experience. For me it came quietly at first. But it comes ever more forcefully each time I have read and prayed over the Book of Mormon.[6]

Elder Boyd K. Packer told a gathering of new mission presidents: "A testimony is not thrust upon you; a testimony grows. We become taller in testimony like we grow taller in physical stature; *we hardly know it happens* because it comes by growth" (emphasis added).[7]

From Elder David A. Bednar:

> I have talked with many individuals who question the strength of their personal testimony and underestimate their spiritual capacity because they do not receive frequent, miraculous, or strong impressions. Perhaps as we consider the experiences of Joseph in the Sacred Grove, of Saul on the road to Damascus, and of Alma the Younger, we come to believe something is wrong with or lacking in us if we fall short in our lives of these well-known and spiritually striking examples. If you have had similar thoughts or doubts, please know that you are quite normal.

Just keep pressing forward obediently and with faith in the Savior. As you do so, you "cannot go amiss" (Doctrine and Covenants 80:3).[8]

From President Dieter F. Uchtdorf to a general priesthood meeting:

Revelation and testimony do not always come with overwhelming force. For many, a testimony comes slowly—a piece at a time. Sometimes it comes so gradually that it is hard to recall the exact moment we actually knew the gospel was true.[9]

So there are volcanic testimonies and sedimentary testimonies, and many types in between. As you reflect on your own testimony, don't get stuck in either/or. Each of has our own way of believing and knowing. Value yours.

"A MIGHTY CHANGE OF HEART"

Expecting a change of heart in one fell swoop is likewise not realistic. Below are a number of statements from General Authorities about this. As perfectionists, it's critical to our spiritual progress and our peace that this message truly sink in. Words from authoritative sources can help us do this.

Elder Neal A. Maxwell said that the natural man and natural woman do not "go away quickly or quietly." Putting him or her off is a process that takes time and repetition: "Time and again, the new self is pitted against the stubborn old self. Sometimes, just when we think the job is done at last, the old self reminds us that he or she has not fully departed yet."[10]

Not only is a dramatic and swift change of heart unrealistic, it is *uncommon.* Elder D. Todd Christofferson invited us to remember that scriptural examples of dramatic changes of heart, like Alma the Younger's, are "remarkable and not typical."[11] President Ezra Taft Benson made the same point in his 1989 *Ensign* First Presidency Message, saying "we must be cautious" when discussing unusual cases such as Alma the Younger, Paul, Enos, and King Lamoni: "Though they are real and powerful, *they are the exception more than the rule.* For every Paul, for every Enos, and for every King Lamoni, there are hundreds and thousands of people who find the process of repentance much more subtle, much more imperceptible" (emphasis added).[12]

Elder Bruce R. McConkie helps us understand that if we are becoming born again over time and in undramatic ways, we are among the majority.

Being born again is a gradual thing, except in a few isolated instances that are so miraculous they get written up in the scriptures. As far as the generality of the members of the Church are concerned, we are born again by degrees, and we are born again to added light and to added knowledge and to added desires for righteousness as we keep the commandments.[13]

Elder Cecil O. Samuelson concurs:

While we believe fully in the mighty change of heart described in the scriptures (see Mosiah 5:2; Alma 5:12–14, 26), we must understand it often occurs gradually, rather than instantaneously or globally, and in response to specific questions, experiences, and concerns as well as by our study and prayer.[14]

President Joseph F. Smith recalls that as a boy he "frequently" asked his Heavenly Father to grant him a testimony by showing him "some marvelous thing." Instead, the Lord showed him line upon line, "until he made me to know the truth from the crown of my head to the soles of my feet, and until doubt and fear had been absolutely purged from me."[15]

Everyday Inspiration and Feeling the Spirit

Even for those who sometimes experience dramatic expressions of the Spirit, everyday promptings and impressions are much more subtle. It helps me in my recovery to remember our leaders' teachings about how the Spirit works in our everyday lives. They have reached a high level of spiritual maturity, and I find their observations and counsel illuminating. Soaking up a variety of expressions at one time can be powerful, so I've compiled below a number of quotes I found particularly enlightening.

The Spirit does not get our attention by shouting or shaking us with a heavy hand. Rather it whispers. It caresses so gently that if we are preoccupied we may not feel it at all.[16]

* * *

As we gain experience with the Holy Ghost, we learn that the intensity with which we feel the Spirit's influence is not always the same. Strong, dramatic spiritual impressions do not come to us frequently. Even as we strive to be faithful and obedient, there simply are times when the direction, assurance, and peace of the Spirit are not readily recognizable in our lives. . .

[T]he Spirit of the Lord usually communicates with us in ways that are quiet, delicate, and subtle.[17]

* * *

As we seek answers from God, we feel the still, small voice whisper to our spirits. These feelings—these impressions—are so natural and so subtle that we may overlook them or attribute them to reason or intuition.[18]

* * *

The voice of the Spirit comes as a *feeling* rather than a sound. You will learn, as I have learned, to "listen" for that voice that is *felt* rather than *heard*. . . . The gift of the Holy Ghost . . . is a spiritual voice that comes into the mind as a thought or a feeling put into your heart.[19]

* * *

Expecting the spectacular, one may not be fully alerted to the constant flow of revealed communication.[20]

* * *

The patterns of revelation are not dramatic. The voice of inspiration is a still voice, a small voice. There need be no trance, no sanctimonious declaration. It is quieter and simpler than that.[21]

* * *

We as members of the Church tend to emphasize marvelous and dramatic spiritual manifestations so much that we may fail to appreciate and may even overlook the customary pattern by which the Holy Ghost accomplishes His work. The very "simpleness of the way" (1 Nephi 17:41) of receiving small and incremental spiritual impressions that over time and in totality constitute a desired answer or the direction we need may cause us to look "beyond the mark" (Jacob 4:14).

We may not see angels, hear heavenly voices, or receive overwhelming spiritual impressions. We frequently may press forward hoping and praying—but without absolute assurance—that we are acting in accordance with God's will. But as we honor our covenants and keep the commandments, as we strive ever more consistently to do good and to become better, we can walk with the confidence that God will guide our steps.[22]

NOTES

1. J. Devn Cornish, "The Privilege of Prayer," *Ensign*, November 2011, 101.

2. Ezra Taft Benson, "Seek the Spirit of the Lord," *Ensign*, April 1988.

3. Carlos A. Godoy, "Testimony as a Process," *Ensign*, November 2008.

4. Ibid., 102.

5. Dallin H. Oaks, "Elder Oaks Interview Transcript from PBS Documentary," Mormon Newsroom news release dated July 20, 2007, retrieved June 23, 2012, from http://www.mormonnewsroom.org/article/elder-oaks-interview-transctipt-from-pbs-documentary.

6. Henry B. Eyring, "A Living Testimony," *Ensign*, May 2011, 126–27.

7. Boyd K. Packer, "The Candle of the Lord," *Ensign*, January 1983.

8. David A. Bednar, "The Spirit of Revelation," *Ensign*, May 2011, 88.

9. Dieter F. Uchtdorf, "Your Potential, Your Privilege," *Ensign*, May 2011, 59, 60.

10. Neal A. Maxwell, "Becoming a Disciple," *Ensign*, June 1996.

11. Christofferson, "Born Again," *Ensign*, May 2008, 78.

12. Ezra Taft Benson, "A Mighty Change of Heart," *Ensign*, October 1989.

13. McConkie, "Jesus Christ and Him Crucified," in *1976 Devotional Speeches of the Year* (Provo, UT: Brigham Young Univeristy Press, 1977), 399.

14. Cecil O. Samuelson, Jr., "Testimony," *Ensign*, May 2011, 41.

15. Joseph F. Smith, quoted in David A. Bednar, "The Spirit of Revelation," *Ensign*, May 2011.

16. Packer, "The Candle of the Lord."

17. Bednar, "That We May Always Have His Spirit to Be with Us," *Ensign*, May 2006.

18. Paul B. Piper, "To Hold Sacred," *Ensign*, May 2012, 111.

19. Packer, "Counsel to Youth," *Ensign*, November 2011, 17–18; emphasis in original.

20. Spencer W. Kimball, "Revelation: The Word of the Lord to His Prophets," *Ensign*, May 1977.

21. Packer, "Revelation in a Changing World," *Ensign*, November 1989.

22. Bednar, "The Spirit of Revelation," *Ensign*, May 2011, 88.

BREATHER

Being Patient with Ourselves

*C*hange is a process. It takes time to absorb insights, experiment with them, and gradually integrate them into our everyday thinking and behavior. Be patient with yourself as you work on lessening your perfectionism.

When you're tempted to chastise yourself because you're not changing as fast as you think you should, remember that you wouldn't expect a beloved child to learn to walk in one day. As she learned, you wouldn't sit on the couch with your arms folded and scold her as she stumbled toward you, got up, and fell again. You would beckon her, help her up, speak encouraging words, and remind her to try again tomorrow.

Your Heavenly Father and your Savior want to do the same for you. Let them.

CHAPTER 13

Being Still

In this fast-paced life, do we ever pause for moments of meditation—even thoughts of timeless truths?

—*President Thomas S. Monson[1]*

 friend of mine tells a story about his father sharing an office with his business partner in a fast-growing enterprise. Every so often when things would get hectic, his father noticed that his partner would disappear. My friend remembers:

> Phones would go unanswered. Tasks went undone. Finally one day in exasperation, Dad searched the building to find out what was going on. In the farthest corner of the warehouse, away from any ringing phone or demanding customer at the front counter, he found his partner painting the workbench. The workbench had dozens of coats of paint, all different. To this day, some forty years later, everyone in the company knows what it means when someone says, "Go paint the workbench."

Sitting still and doing nothing—or doing something that *appears* useless—is tough for perfectionistic folks. We want to be doing and accomplishing and achieving all the time. We know we're supposed to stop and smell the roses, but when we try, we zoom in on the weeds and have to pull them first. After perfecting the scene, we might have time for a quick whiff but don't linger to truly take in the fragrance and splendor of the flowers. Too often we end up deprived of a valuable moment of refreshment.

RESIGNING OUR MEMBERSHIP IN THE CULT OF SPEED

We've all heard a thousand times about our unhealthy super fast North American culture. You know the phrases—"the frantic pace of modern life," "our rush-rush world," "hurry up and slow down," "life in the fast lane," "always on the go," "overworked and stressed out." Perfectionists are especially vulnerable to cultural voices that tell us we're not doing enough if we're not super busy, overscheduled, and frantically working toward goals. We also tend to use busyness as way to make sure we look like we're valuable. If our to-do list is long, it means we're in demand and thus we must be adequate and worthy. It's a cover-up for not understanding what ails us or what to do about it.

In Anne Morrow Lindbergh's deeply spiritual book about moving away from speed and toward contemplation, *Gift from the Sea*, she aptly describes this coping style: "Not knowing how to feed the spirit, we try to muffle its demands in distractions. Instead of stilling the center, the axis of the wheel, we add more centrifugal activities to our lives—which tend to throw us off balance."[2] (And lest we think the cult of speed is a recent "innovation," the first edition of Lindbergh's book was published in 1955.)

To perceive the quiet center of our being that our spirit craves, we have to slow down. To hear and feel the soft and quiet voice of the Spirit, we have to slow down. To gain the insights we need to gently make course corrections, we have to slow down.

Sister Vicki F. Matsumori of the Primary general presidency counseled during October 2009 general conference: "If we provide a still and quiet time each day when we are not bombarded by television, computer, video games, or personal electronic devices, we allow that still, small voice an opportunity to provide personal revelation and to whisper sweet guidance, reassurance, and comfort to us."[3]

So how does the phrase "waste time" grab you? Anxious and uneasy? Don't the scriptures tell us that "thou shalt not idle away thy time"

(Doctrine and Covenants 60:13)? Aren't we're supposed to be "anxiously engaged" (Doctrine and Covenants 58:26–28)? Yes, of course. The scriptures are true! *And*, at the same time, it's good for perfectionists to slow down and allow themselves to be still.

On a hot summer day, when I sit for awhile under the cool shade of my grape vines, I like to think of it as "wasting time with God," a phrase I borrow from Christian writer and minister Michael Evans, who argues in his book *Why Not Waste Time with God?*[4] that since we all waste at least some time every day, why not spend some of it with God? If you're spending time with God, of course, it's not possible to be wasting your time. But I like the phrase anyway because it reminds me that as a recovering perfectionist, I *need* to be idle sometimes. Maybe idleness is not okay for those more prone to slacking, but for me it's a good thing. In fact, I would argue that anytime a "saint" slows down to reconstitute herself, no matter what's she's doing or not doing, she's spending time with God. For people who are generally diligent, being "idle" and "wasting time" have a righteous purpose. That purpose is to refresh, reconstitute, and reconnect with God. So in fact none of this is wasting time in the slightest.

Elder Dieter F. Uchtdorf spoke of this important principle when he counseled us to slow down, simplify, and focus on the things that matter most—*especially when stress levels rise and when distress appears.*[5] Elder L. Tom Perry did exactly this a number of years ago when his employment became challenging and his wife was diagnosed with a life-threatening illness. At the time, they happened to be living in Massachusetts near the very place that has become a symbol of slowing down and simplifying—Walden Pond. Elder Perry recounts that he and his wife drove to the pond when they needed "to get away for a few moments of relief from our troubles, talk, and give emotional comfort to each other." Sometimes they walked around the pond and other times they sat in the car and talked. "Walden Pond was our special place to pause, reflect, and heal. Perhaps it was partly due to its history—its connection to the efforts of Henry David Thoreau to separate himself from worldliness for a period of years—that Walden Pond offered us so much hope for simplicity and provided such a renewing escape from our overly complex lives."[6]

I submit to you that as someone with perfectionistic tendencies, your stress levels are almost always high, and you are almost always feeling distressed. As you gently steer onto a less perfectionistic path, it's particularly important for you to slow down.

Some of the things I do to slow down include:

- When I visit a particular assisted living facility for my job, I often stop at its duck pond and sit for awhile. I take in the beauty of the setting, the sounds of the ducks, and the sweetness of elderly men and women watching along with me.

- When I'm about to cook brown rice, I'll pour it onto a plate and slowly pick out the too-green kernels, using my fingers like a rake and handling the kernels like grains of sand in a Zen garden.

- I brush my long-haired cat as long as she wants (usually quite a while).

- During a family party that gets loud and chaotic, sometimes I plant myself on the couch and watch the little ones intently, taking in their quirks, their words, and the pure innocence of their faces.

- When shopping at a store that I enjoy, I'll move slowly and put things in my cart that I like. I'll "own" them for awhile, acknowledge that I don't need them, and return them to their proper places.

I asked my friends and family to tell me about how they slow down, and here are some of their answers:

- I drive the speed limit on the freeway. It is amazing how relaxing it is to let everybody else zip around you as if they are madly dashing toward some never-to-be-reached finish line while you are just calmly driving along. Plus I have the extra peace of knowing I'll never get stopped for speeding.

- On Fridays I get off work early, so sometimes rather than head to my heavily occupied home (kids, grandkids, furkids) I usually go to a movie. I go to the matinee so it costs less, and I get popcorn and indulge in soda (which I rarely do) and totally escape for a couple of hours.

- This year on the day before Easter, the pressure was increasing with my inventor son's contraption and the debris of creation littering the yard and patio where the family dinner and egg hunt were still to be hosted. To take the pressure off, I spent most of the day before digging in the dirt in the front yard. The neighbor stopped by to see what I was planting. Nothing. Just digging.

- I seldom listen to the radio when I'm in the car. I take this time to meditate.

- I work in my garden. I take great pleasure in the colors and diversity. I like to hear the kids playing outside and feel the sun on my face.

- I like to rummage through thrift stores like Goodwill and Salvation Army in search of accidental fortunes.

- I used to be a production manager in manufacturing, and my mind was always going full speed ahead. I thought stress was the norm. It frustrated me big time to sit and wait for the ferry to get home from work when I commuted, so I bought a motorcycle since they boarded first. When my back condition no longer allowed me to work full-time, I had some adjustments to make. Time is different for me now. I'm no longer in a rush all the time. I can stop and smell the roses. I can now sit on the ferry and just enjoy the scenery without having a project I'm working on every second.

- Breathe. Just breathe. It's amazing how focusing on your breath can help to center you. It makes me aware of where in my body I am tense and then I can let it go.

- Fishing is always good. Catching not so much. It's the outdoor commune with nature that gives me peace and a recalibrated sense of what is real.

BEING STILL TO LISTEN FOR GOD

If we know it's good for us to slow down for the sake of our exhausted bodies and worn out minds, it's logical to realize how even more important it is for us to slow down so we can listen for God. Sometimes we're so intent on getting through our checklist each day that we forget how easy it is to sidestep the *how* of reading the scriptures, the *how* of praying, the *how* of doing our visiting teaching and home teaching. I'm embarrassed to admit how often I don't feel like praying but do it anyway only because I know I'll feel guilty if I don't. When I get up off my knees after these perfunctory prayers, I'll think, "Well, at least I was obedient," and my guilt is assuaged.

Are my thoughts in the paragraph above a failure to be gentle with myself, which is extra important for me as a recovering perfectionist? Isn't a perfunctory prayer "good enough" sometimes? Yes, it is. It's mostly better to go through the motions from time to time than it is to skip important rituals altogether. I learned this lesson from Eugene England, the late BYU professor whose essay "Why the Church Is as True as the Gospel" has had a profound influence on me. He recalls that as a child he dreaded stake conferences as the "most boring meeting in the Church, perhaps in the world"—but went anyway. When he attended at age twelve, he remembers turning around to tease his sister in the row behind him.

> Suddenly I felt something, vaguely familiar, burning to the center of my heart and bones—and then, it seemed, physically turning me around to look at the transfigured face of Elder Harold B. Lee, the visiting authority. . . . And I became aware . . . of the presence of the Holy Ghost and the special witness of Jesus Christ.
>
> How many boring stake conferences would I attend to be even once in the presence of such grace? Thousands—all there are. That pearl is without price.

And, he emphasizes, this was "an experience I could have had only because I was doing my duty in the Church, however immaturely."[7] I had an experience in the same vein, though not as dramatic, after President Gordon B. Hinckley challenged members of the Church in August 2005 to read the Book of the Mormon before the end of the year. He made an extraordinary promise to those who followed his counsel:

> Without reservation I promise you that if each of you will observe this simple program, regardless of how many times you previously may have read the Book of Mormon, there will come into your lives and into your homes an added measure of the Spirit of the Lord, a strengthened resolution to walk in obedience to His commandments, and a stronger testimony of the living reality of the Son of God.[8]

I was one of those who had read the Book of Mormon many times, and I preferred to read it slowly and carefully. I would have to read quickly to be done in the time frame he suggested. I decided to "do my duty" and obey. I had felt a witness of the book's truthfulness when I was twelve, and I didn't expect much from reading it in a way that didn't fit my personal approach to scripture study. I did it anyway. President Hinckley's promise was fulfilled beyond anything I imagined. As I read quickly and took in these sacred writings in a different, big-gulp way, I saw patterns and themes I had not seen before. The holy messages became concentrated in a way that sent them to the center of my soul. I felt the Spirit so strongly so often when reading during this time that I began to feel the Spirit by simply holding the book in my hand. Now, seven years later, I still feel the blessings promised by President Hinckley, especially "an added measure of the Spirit of the Lord."

So duty is important. Going through the motions can open us up to opportunities that otherwise might never come. It is when we get stuck in duty mode that we put ourselves in spiritual danger. Performing our obligations by will alone, as perfectionists are wont to do, eventually depletes us. If we stay in that mode for any length of time, we burn out and risk giving up altogether. Duty mode is not sustainable.

The Lord wants us to feel the joy that wholehearted engagement brings, not the deadening somnolence of walking in lockstep. It's even possible that staying predominantly in duty mode is more harmful to our spirits than not doing our duty at all. The Savior described just how strongly He feels about the indifference of merely going through the motions: "So then because thou art lukewarm, and neither cold nor hot, I will spue thee out of my mouth" (Revelation 3:16). Lukewarm-ness, it appears, doesn't just prevent us from growing spiritually. It actually makes us move backwards *because it separates us from God.*

So what does all this have to do with being still to listen for God? Why would being still help me be wholeheartedly engaged? If I want to engage my whole heart, don't I have to *do* something? Doesn't being engaged mean getting up *off* my chair and *acting*?

My answer: It's almost impossible to be still and be lukewarm. Sitting still to commune with God is the opposite of mindlessly going through the motions. It's mind-*full*. It's motion-*less*.

Sitting still doesn't always mean finding a quiet place, closing your eyes, and waiting to feel God's presence. Sometimes it's sitting still at chaotic family picnic and watching for God amidst the commotion. You might see a sky so blue it makes your heart ache. God is in that. You might see a child climb onto Grandpa's lap and look up at him with shining eyes. God is in that. You might see a bird fly to a nest and feed her babies. God is in that. You might see a dog wag her tail adoringly as her master comes into view. God is in that. You might perceive more acutely your own longing to be closer to the Lord. God is in your yearning.

When we're waiting and being still and listening, are we striving? No. Are we seeking approval? No. Stillness allows us to be in the moment. We don't regret the past. We don't worry about the future. We just *are*. And it's when we just *are* that the most amazing things happen. As you are still more often and frantic less often, you will find your spiritual appetite increasing. Rather than the unappetizing repellence of lockstep conformity to what's expected of you, you begin to hunger and thirst to do good and be good (Matthew 5:6). You'll find yourself wanting more than spiritual crumbs. You'll yearn to feast upon His word (2 Nephi 31:20; 32:3)—and upon His love (Jacob 3:2).

> *Thy words were found, and I did eat them; and thy word was unto me the joy and rejoicing of mine heart. (Jeremiah 15:16)*

MEDITATION FOR PERFECTIONISTS

I have tried many times over the years to establish a personal meditation practice. I've taken a course in transcendental meditation, a seminar in the yogic Sudarshan Kriya breathing technique, and a workshop on Mormon Meditation. I've read books about meditation, listened to meditation tapes and CDs, and set my white noise machine to ocean sounds. None of it "took" for any length of time. I kept trying in my perfectionistic determination to meditate correctly. If I did, I thought, maybe I would feel closer to God.

If any of the more formal meditation techniques work for you, that's great. Keep using them! If you're like me and they don't, I have three simple phrases for you:

- Close your eyes.

- Sit still.

- Breathe slowly.

If you want to get slightly more complicated, choose a word or phrase that is meaningful to you and focus on it as you breathe. I have used *Jesus* and *peace*. As thoughts impinge, gently redirect yourself to the word or phrase.

That's it. You really don't have to do any more than those three things to get to a place where your mind slows down and your spirit tunes in.

Notes

1.   Thomas S. Monson, "The Race of Life," *Ensign*, May 2012, 90.

2.   Anne Morrow Lindbergh, *Gift from the Sea*, 20th ed. (New York: Random House / Vintage Books, 1978), 52.

3.   Vicki F. Matsumori, "Helping Others Recognize the Whisperings of the Spirit," *Ensign*, November 2009, 10

4.   Michael Evans, *Why Not Waste Time with God? Moving Beyond a Superficial Relationship with God to Live in Intimacy with Him* (Winter Park, FL: Archer-Ellison Publishing Company, 2003).

5.   Dieter F. Uchtdorf, "Of Things That Matter Most," *Ensign*, November 2010, 19.

6.   L. Tom Perry, "Let Him Do It with Simplicity," *Ensign*, November 2008, 7.

7.   Eugene England, in *Readings for Intensive Writers*, 3rd ed. (Boston: Pearson Custom Publishing, 2002), Susan T. Laing, Compiler, 166, 167.

8.   Gordon B. Hinckley, "A Testimony Vibrant and True," *Ensign*, August 2005.

BREATHER

A Note on Perfectionism versus Slackerism

As I worked on this book, I discussed it with a number of people. From the beginning, one friend consistently argued that the premise of my book is wrong. He believes that in general Latter-day Saints are not too hard on themselves but rather are not hard enough on themselves. There's no way to know if this assessment is correct since no one knows what percentage of Latter-day Saints are perfectionistic and what percentage are slackers—and how would one assess this anyway? Whatever the percentages, this book is aimed at those who tend toward perfectionism. For us, I have a few thoughts on this topic.

- We all have both the over-doer and the slacker in us. Some lean more often one way than the other. If you're reading this book, chances are you lean more often toward over-doing. It's good to identify that about yourself so you're more likely to recognize times when you might need to gently guide yourself back into balance. But we can all err on both sides. If you're not good at judging this yourself, ask people you trust to help you know which side you're erring on.

- Perfectionists are prone to wild swings between being meticulously conscientious and wanting to throw it all away and be rebellious and irresponsible. It's like the deprivation response that occurs with dieting. When you deprive yourself of foods you love for an extended period, chances are high you'll binge on those foods at some point. What follows is guilt, shame, and a renewed determination to "be good" about eating. But if "being good" means only deprivation, it's not sustainable.

- Similarly, when you drive yourself relentlessly toward achievement and goals and deprive yourself of rest and replenishment, chances are high you'll collapse and fall into forced slacking off. You then will likely judge yourself as being a slacker and feel guilt, shame, and a renewed determination to push yourself to your (unreasonable) limits. Again, not sustainable.

- One of the better solutions to dieting exhaustion is to gently guide yourself toward a more natural style of eating where you recognize true hunger rather than swing between depriving yourself and over-indulging. Similarly, an alternative to perfectionistic exhaustion is to gently guide yourself to toward a more natural style of effort where you recognize your hunger for being more like Christ and balance your efforts toward that aspiration with rest—rather than swing between relentless effort and giving up. We've already covered that in more detail in the chapter about being still.

- Accept that you're going to be imperfect at finding just the right balance all the time between legitimately working hard at important things and taking time for renewal. Let the Lord help you as you seek that balance.

- Slacking is not always a bad thing. As we learned in strategy 1, words have great power, and "slacking" or "slacker" are on the self-judgmental side. Better words for the times you need to "slack off" are *resting, relaxing, refreshing, renewing, replenishing.* Think of them as "R" words.

- Be gentle with yourself.

SUMMARY OF STRATEGY 3

*E*nlisting the Savior as your chief ally is *the* key step as you endeavor to ease perfectionistic tendencies. His arm is outstretched to you always, and it's up to you to receive Him. Receiving and accepting his invitation might include the following:

- More deeply understanding what it means to spiritually receive.

- Showing your willingness to receive by singing and reciting scriptures aloud.

- Paying attention to the special hazards of repenting for perfectionists:

    - Seeing repentance as a one-time event rather than an ongoing process.

    - Getting stuck in remorse.

    - Avoiding repentance when it means others might see you as less than perfect.

    - Failing to forgive yourself.

    - Not believing the Atonement is for you personally.

- Moderating expectations about testimony, praying, and feeling the Spirit.

- Creating a personal approach for handling anxiety-provoking scriptures.

- Slowing down and being still.

CHAPTER 14

Embracing Your Perfectly Imperfect Self

I dreamt a few nights ago that I had the task of tilling a *hillside. I was struggling with this old hand plow—one of those metal ones with a wheel and a pronged claw. The soil was hard and rocky, and the sun was scorching hot. I was toiling and grinding, and the sweat was pouring down my face. My muscles ached, and I felt like I was going to crumple any minute, but for some reason I couldn't stop or even slow down. I completed a row, turned around, and began plowing another row a few steps higher, dreading every step ahead. Suddenly an angelic being appeared in front of me and extended her palm toward me in a gesture that clearly said "Stop!"*

I stopped, stunned.

She spoke in the most soft and gentle voice.

"It isn't this hard."

And then she was gone.

I dropped to the ground, flooded with relief and release and utter joy.

I didn't have to work that hard.

I was the one who had decided I had to labor like that.

It took a message from heaven to convince me that I didn't.

I heard a woman relate this dream many years ago during a gathering of women when I lived in the Los Angeles area. I don't remember her name or much about her, but the dream was unforgettable. It struck me to my core and became an important piece in facing my perfectionism. I decided to co-opt the dream as my own, and you can do that too if it's helpful.

As you use what works for you in the preceding chapters and walk your own path toward embracing your imperfect self, please consider these ideas.

Imperfections are Gifts—Be Grateful for Them

The journey toward becoming more like our Savior requires that we experience imperfections both in ourselves and in those around us. It's part of His plan that we experience imperfect parenting as helpless infants, resulting in psychic wounds that provide us with a lifetime of learning—if we use them. It's part of His plan that imperfect biology gives us physical challenges to cope with. It's part of His plan that our weaknesses (inborn or learned) such as arrogance, quickness to anger, laziness, or passiveness, mean we will hurt others and need their forgiveness.

- Why would we desire to be humble unless we're sometimes cocky and experience how that imperfection hurts our spirits and others'?

- Why would we want to become less judgmental if we've never felt the sting of realizing our criticism has injured a loved one?

- Why would we be motivated to learn how to forgive if we've never needed to be forgiven?

Our imperfections can be our friends by pointing us toward our distinctive path of progress toward eternal life. Resist begrudging the very things that will bring you closer to your Savior as you enlist Him to help you. Though you might whine a bit about your shortcomings and about spiritual strengths you wish you had, don't stay there long. Be like Alma, who wished he were an angel and could cry repentance "with the voice of thunder," but who quickly realized he was a man and "ought to be content with the things which Lord hath allotted unto [him]" (Alma 29:1–3).

Be Okay with Muddling Through

A wise counselor taught me that I don't have to plan everything, obsess about what-ifs before a performance, process endlessly a failure or perceived failure, or imagine worst-case scenarios and prepare ad infinitum against them. "Just muddle through," he would say. The first few times he used that phrase, I sputtered lots of "but-but-buts." Really? I can be a conscientious disciple of Christ and just muddle? It took awhile for me to accept that, but when I did, it was incredibly freeing.

Imagine my delight when in January 2012, a friend posted on Facebook that she had just heard an Apostle speak to a professional group, and during the question-and-answer session he responded to the last question—how one can balance career, family, church, and community service—with the following: "I just muddle through it."

You too can muddle through.

Value "Becoming"

Our Church culture is shifting from an emphasis on works and doing to a balance between both doing and being. I see evidence of this in general conference, lesson manuals, policies, and talks in local meetings. At our ward conference in 2012, our stake president ended his talk by telling us: "I'm grateful for all that you are and for who you're trying to become."

In some ways, being is harder than doing, though neither is easy. A friend raised this thoughtful question:

> How do we deal with ever-rising understandings of what is expected of us? As we move from dealing with the more obvious temptations to understanding that not just our actions but our motives and hearts must be right, we have even more to feel guilty about. As I understand more that this earth life is supposed to focus not just on doing but on being, I see the vast gulf that separates who I am from who I should be.

I hope helpful answers are within these pages. As we draw more and more upon the atoning power of Jesus Christ, He will help us move from one level of spiritual maturity to the next. Even as we gradually come to understand that more is required of us than we anticipated, He will be with us.

WHEN YOU'RE SCARED OR ANXIOUS BECAUSE OF MISTAKES, SINS, AND UGLY FEELINGS, TURN IT TO LOVE

Because love is the great commandment, it ought to be at the center of all and everything we do in our own family, in our Church callings, and in our livelihood. . . . Love is the fire that warms our lives with unparalleled joy and divine hope. Love should be our walk and our talk.

—Dieter F. Uchtdorf [1]

In March 2012, I came upon an article in the *Church News* with the headline "Love: Most Powerful Force." It reported on a devotional at Brigham Young University, and the speaker asked the students:

"What if our only motive was love?

"What if everything we did, we did out of love?"

The questions stayed with me. Might they be useful to perfectionists who struggle with guilt, anxiety, and self-loathing?

The speaker, Sunday School general president Russell T. Osguthorpe, also told students, according to the article, that "in the long run, why they do things is probably more important than what they do." [2]

In other words, our thoughts—the words we say to ourselves—are on equal footing with what we actually do. Words matter! Since most perfectionistic angst comes from inside our heads, what would happen if every time we felt anxious and scared because we fear being or appearing imperfect, we turned our thoughts to love. What I'm suggesting is an inner dialogue something like this, using myself as an example:

> Right now I'm writing the last few pages of this book that means so much to me. Once the words are in print, it's forever. If I embarrass myself with too much self-disclosure or some line of thinking that's half-baked, it will be there for all to see. There are some people out there who might want to take me down a peg or two, and I can just see them pointing to some dumb thing I wrote and laughing at it.
>
> Wait! Stop! Why am I writing this book? I'm writing it out of love. I'm hoping at least a few people will find healing from their perfectionism as I have. If someone finds ammunition against me in these pages, they're spiritually unevolved. Stop again! If I want everything I do to be out of love, then I want to be loving toward my critics too.

As I wrote out the first paragraph, my anxiety started to rise. I could feel each fear build on itself. One scary thought led to another, and worst-case scenarios started to bubble up. When I stopped myself and replaced the self-injuring thoughts with loving thoughts, the anxiety diminished. Then the loving thoughts began to trigger loving feelings.

The relief didn't hold for very long, I have to admit. The what-ifs wormed their way back in, and I had to start over. It takes awareness, energy, and discipline to keep the wounding thoughts away, and we don't always have enough reserves to keep this process going. And that's the point. We try, we ask for God's help, we try again, we rest from trying, and we're gentle and loving toward ourselves throughout it all.

Ultimately, it is our love for Christ and His love for us that give us the resilience to keep trying—and the purest and most powerful motives. The more we love Him and receive His love for us, the more we love ourselves and others. The more our souls enlarge with His perfect love, the less we need to hide our flaws, sins, and imperfections. Because we are so profoundly loved, we feel free to bring them out into the open, confident that the wounds they've created in us and in others will be treated with the most tender care. When we no longer cover our imperfectness with fear, anxiety, and shame but choose to open them to the Light, we can receive the healing power of His Atonement and His love.

We can't produce this pure love of Christ by our own will. They are gifts from Him, the fount of all goodness. With all the energy of our hearts, we can pray for Christ's pure love, humbly receive it, share it, and "be filled" (Moroni 7:48).

NOTES

1.   Dieter F. Uchtdorf, "The Love of God," *Ensign*, November 2009, 21.

2.   Russell T. Osguthorpe, "Love: Most Powerful Force," *Church News*, March 12, 2011, 15.

SEEKING A COUNSELOR

$\mathcal{S}$ome of you are likely wondering if counseling might be a good idea. If you aren't sure one way or the other, think about these questions:

- Am I having trouble coping with everyday life?

- Have I tried to solve my problems on my own for awhile now but not made any significant progress?

- Has more than one person suggested that I get professional help?

If you answered yes to any one of these questions, then it's likely time to consult a professional. To find a good one:

- Pray for help finding the right person to work with you.

- Ask for recommendations from trusted friends, Church leaders, teachers, and doctors.

- Check the Church's Provident Living website (www.provident living.org) to see if LDS Family Services is available in your area.

- Interview possible counselors before agreeing to meet. Questions might include:

  – Are you licensed?

  – What are your fees?

  – What if I don't have insurance?

– Do you have experience treating people who are perfectionistic?

– Do you integrate spirituality with psychological principles?

– [If not LDS] What is your perspective about Latter-day Saints?

The first few times you meet with a counselor, remember that you're a paying client, and you have a right to feel comfortable with the person who is advising you about your life. If at any time you feel a counselor does not respect and honor your values, you should not continue. But be sure to consider whether your discomfort might come from the counselor encouraging you to honestly examine your values. If the latter is likely, consider this advice from Allen E. Bergin, PhD, an expert on what makes psychotherapy effective or ineffective: "Tolerate the temporary distress and work to articulate what you truly believe. Good therapists, whether Latter-day Saint or non-Latter-day-Saint, can help you discern between behavior that legitimately follows from doctrine as opposed to behavior that might appear doctrinal but in reality could be a harmful cultural prescription."[1]

He cautions further: "Unfortunately, professional standards for state licensure are uneven. Many poorly trained therapists are able to practice. If a therapist seems aggressive, intrusive, cold, or eccentric, seek another therapist."[2]

NOTES

1.   Allen E. Bergin, *Eternal Values and Personal Growth: A Guide on Your Journey to Spiritual, Emotional and Social Wellness* (Provo, Utah: BYU Studies, 2002), 25.

2.   Ibid., 26.

APPENDIX

Comforting Thoughts for Perfectionists

SCRIPTURES

Peace I leave with you, my peace I give unto you: . . . Let not your heart be troubled, neither let it be afraid. (John 14:27)

* * *

Come unto Christ, and be perfected *in him*, and deny yourselves of all ungodliness; . . . and love God with all your might, mind and strength, . . . that by his grace ye may be perfect in Christ. (Moroni 10:32; emphasis added)

* * *

Be faithful and diligent . . . and I will encircle thee in the arms of my love. (Doctrine and Covenants 6:20).

* * *

Come unto me, all ye that labor and are heavy laden, and I will give you rest. Take my yoke upon you, and learn of me; for I am meek and lowly in heart: and ye shall find rest unto your souls. For my yoke is easy, and my burden is light. (Matthew 11:28–30)

* * *

And see that all these things are done in wisdom and order; for it is not requisite that a man should run faster than he has strength. And again, it is expedient that he should be diligent, that thereby he might win the prize; therefore, all things must be done in order. (Mosiah 4:27)

* * *

Do not run faster or labor more than you have strength and means . . . but be diligent unto the end. (Doctrine and Covenants 10:4)

* * *

Now is the time and the day of your salvation; and therefore, if ye will repent, and harden not your hearts, immediately shall the great plan of redemption be brought about unto you. (Alma 34:30–31)

* * *

I am able to make you holy, and your sins are forgiven you. (Doctrine and Covenants 60:7)

* * *

Now they, after being sanctified by the Holy Ghost, having their garments made white, being pure and spotless before God, could not look upon sin save it were with abhorrence; and there were *many, exceeding great many,* who were made pure and entered into the rest of the Lord their God. (emphasis added) (Alma 13:11–12).

* * *

Therefore, sanctify yourselves that your minds become single to God, and the days will come that you shall see him; for he will unveil his face unto you, and it shall be in his own time, and in his own way, and according to his own will. (Doctrine and Covenants 88:68)

CHURCH LEADERS

We all need to remember: men are that they might have joy—not guilt trips!

—Elder Russell M. Nelson

"Perfection Pending," *Ensign*, November 1995, 86.

APPENDIX

The Church is "for the perfecting of the saints" (Ephesians 4:12); it is not a well-provisioned rest home for the already perfected.

—Elder Neal A. Maxwell

"A Brother Offended," *Ensign*, May 1982, 38.

We have to become perfect to be saved in the celestial kingdom, but nobody becomes perfect in this life. Only the Lord Jesus attained that state, and he had an advantage that none of us has. He was the Son of God. . . . Becoming perfect in Christ is a process.

—Elder Bruce R. McConkie

1976 Devotional Speeches of the Year
(Provo: Brigham Young University Press, 1977), 399–400.

It occurs to me that there are probably hundreds or even thousands who do not understand what worthiness is. Worthiness is a process, and perfection is an eternal trek. We can be worthy to enjoy certain privileges without being perfect. . . . We need to come to terms with our desire to reach perfection and our frustration when our accomplishments or behaviors are less than perfect. I feel that one of the great myths we would do well to dispel is that we've come to earth to perfect ourselves, and nothing short of that will do. If I understand the teachings of the prophets of this dispensation correctly, we will not become perfect in this life, though we can make significant strides toward that goal.

—Elder Marvin J. Ashton

"On Being Worthy," *Ensign*, May 1989, 20.

Now, this is the truth. We humble people, we who feel ourselves sometimes so worthless, so good-for-nothing, we are not so worthless as we think. There is not one of us but what God's love has been expended upon. There is not one of us that He has not cared for and caressed. There is not one of us that He has not desired to save and that He has not devised means to save. There is not one of us that He has not given His angels charge concerning. We may be insignificant and contemptible in our own eyes and in the eyes of others, but the truth remains that we are children of God and that He has actually given His angels . . . charge concerning us, and they watch over us and have us in their keeping.

—President George Q. Cannon

Gospel Truths, comp. Jerreld L. Newquist, 2 vols.
(Salt Lake City: Deseret Book, 1974), 1:2.

I speak, not to the slackers in the Kingdom, but to those who carry their own load and more; not to those lulled into false security, but to those buffeted by false insecurity, who, though laboring devotedly in the Kingdom, have recurring feelings of falling forever short. . . .

The first thing to be said of this feeling of inadequacy is that it is normal. . . . Following celestial road signs while in telestial traffic jams is not easy, especially when we are not just moving next door—or even across town.

—Elder Neal A. Maxwell

"Notwithstanding My Weakness," *Ensign*, November 1976, 12.

Perfection is worth striving for even if it is ultimately unattainable in this life. For it is through our struggle to become like the Savior and His Father that we ourselves become perfected. If we follow the pattern that Christ set for us, we will be responding to the scriptural mandate to "come unto Christ, and be perfected in him" (Moroni 10:32).

—Elder Joseph B. Wirthlin

"Guided by His Exemplary Life," *Ensign*, February 1999, 34.

I do not ask that you reach beyond your capacity. Please don't nag yourself with thoughts of failure. Do not set goals far beyond your capacity to achieve. Simply do what you can do, in the best way you know, and the Lord will accept of your effort.

—President Gordon B. Hinckley

"Rise to the Stature of the Divine within You," *Ensign*, November 1989, 94.

APPENDIX

"Be ye therefore perfect" (Matthew 5:48), our Savior's admonition in the Sermon on the Mount, is of great concern for many of us as we try to reconcile our lives with this important counsel. Yet the teachings of Jesus Christ are for those of us who are imperfect. To the Pharisees' question about why He ate with publicans and sinners, Christ replied: "They that be whole need not a physician, but they that are sick" (Matthew 9:12). What a blessing to know that the focus of his work is with imperfect people!

—Elder LeGrand R. Curtis

"Perfection: A Daily Process," *Ensign*, July 1995, 30.

There are things that most of us will need to work on throughout our entire lives and yet not reach the perfection that is eventually promised until the eternities if we are true and faithful. Matters such as having absolute faith in the Lord Jesus Christ, a complete understanding of the scriptures, always controlling our thoughts and our tongues are all issues that require persistence and patience. . . . Be sure that you do not have higher standards for yourself or others than the Lord has established. Find satisfaction in your progress while acknowledging that perfection may still be distant.

—Elder Cecil O. Samuelson

"What Does It Mean to Be Perfect?" From a devotional given on March 19, 2002, at the Provo Missionary Training Center.

As we move towards perfection, it is easy to feel that we fall short. We can take confidence that the Lord knows us intimately; He knows the intent of our hearts. He will surely show us the way as we humble ourselves, are obedient, and work toward continual improvement. Even now, He prepares us in ways that we can't yet see. The eyes of our understanding will be opened as we keep the commandments and seek to serve Him. We have the potential to eventually become perfected in Christ. This is a divine inheritance.

—Elder Dale E. Miller

"The Kingdom's Perfecting Pathway," *Ensign*, May 1998, 29.

In urging us to be perfect as our Father in Heaven is perfect, Jesus was not taunting us or teasing us. He was telling us a powerful truth about our possibilities and about our potential. It is a truth almost too stunning to contemplate. Jesus, who could not lie, sought to beckon us to move further along the pathway to perfection. . . . The scriptures contain many marvelous case studies of leaders who, unlike Jesus, were not perfect but were still very effective.

—President Spencer W. Kimball

"Jesus: The Perfect Leader," *Ensign,* August 1979, 5.

Salvation does not come all at once; we are commanded to be perfect even as our Father in heaven is perfect. It will take us ages to accomplish this end, for there will be greater progress beyond the grave, and it will be there that the faithful will overcome all things, and receive all things, even the fullness of the Father's glory. I believe the Lord meant just what he said: that we should be perfect, as our Father in heaven is perfect. That will not come all at once, but line upon line, and precept upon precept, example upon example, and even then not as long as we live in this mortal life, for we will have to go even beyond the grave before we reach that perfection and shall be like God. But here we lay the foundation.

—Elder Joseph Fielding Smith

Doctrines of Salvation, 3 vols., comp. Bruce R. McConkie
(Salt Lake City: Deseret Book, 1954–56), 2:18.

What we do in this life is chart a course leading to eternal life. That course begins here and now and continues in the realms ahead. We must determine in our hearts and in our souls, with all the power and ability we have, that from this time forward we will press on in righteousness; by so doing we can go where God and Christ are. If we make that firm determination, and are in the course of our duty when this life is over, we will continue in that course in eternity. That same spirit that possesses our bodies at the time we depart from this mortal life will have power to possess our bodies in the eternal world. If we go out of this life loving the Lord, desiring righteousness, and seeking to acquire the attributes of godliness, we will have that same spirit in the eternal world, and we will then continue to advance and progress until an ultimate, destined day when we will possess, receive, and inherit all things.

—Elder Bruce R. McConkie

"The Seven Deadly Heresies," in *Speeches of the Year, 1980*
(Provo, Utah: Brigham Young University, 1981), 78–79.

Somehow, some of us get it in our heads that if we are not making great, dramatic leaps forward spiritually, we are not progressing. Actually, for most of us, the challenge of living the gospel is that progress comes in almost imperceptible increments. It is very seldom that we can look back over one day and see great progress. Becoming like God takes years and years of striving, and trying again.

—Gerald N. Lund

"I Have a Question," *Ensign*, August 1986, 38–41.

What good is it to have a Savior if no one is saved? It's like having a lifeguard that won't get out of the chair. The great truth of the gospel is that we have a Savior who can and will save us from ourselves, from what we lack, from our imperfections, from the carnality within us, if we seek his help. . . . Many of us are trying to save ourselves, holding the Atonement of Jesus Christ at arm's distance and saying, "When I've perfected myself, then I'll be worthy of the Atonement." But that's not how it works. That's like saying, "I won't take the medicine until I'm well. I'll be worthy of it then."

—Stephen E. Robinson

"Believing Christ," *Ensign*, April 1992, 5.

In Matthew 5:48, the term perfect was translated from the Greek *teleios*, which means "complete." *Teleios* is an adjective derived from the noun *telos*, which means "end." The infinitive form of the verb is *teleiono*, which means "to reach a distant end, to be fully developed, to consummate, or to finish." Please note that the word does not imply "freedom from error"; it implies "achieving a distant objective." In fact, when writers of the Greek New Testament wished to describe perfection of behavior—precision or excellence of human effort—they did not employ a form of teleios; instead, they chose different words. . . . Such lofty standards, when *earnestly pursued*, produce great inner peace and incomparable joy. . . . Let us do the best we can and try to improve each day. When our imperfections appear, we can keep trying to correct them. We can be more forgiving of flaws in ourselves and among those we love. We can be comforted and forbearing. The Lord taught, "Ye are not able to abide the presence of God now . . . ; wherefore, continue in patience until ye are perfected."

Elder Russell M. Nelson

"Perfection Pending," *Ensign*, November 1995, 86 (emphasis added).

We will not become perfect in a day or a month or a year. We will not accomplish it in a lifetime, but we can keep trying, starting with our more obvious weaknesses and gradually converting them to strengths as we go forward with our lives. "Look to God, and live" (Alma 37:47). Kneel before Him in supplication. He will help you. He will bless you. He will comfort and sustain you. There will be progress. There will be growth. There will be improvement. And there will be much of added happiness. . . . If there has been failure in the past, if there has been sin, if there has been indolence, they may all be overcome.

—President Gordon B. Hinckley

"The Quest for Excellence," *Ensign*, September 1999, 2.

I feel that [the Savior] will give that punishment which is the very least that our transgression will justify. I believe that he will bring into his justice all of the infinite love and blessing and mercy and kindness and understanding which he has. . . .

And on the other hand, I believe that when it comes to making the rewards for our good conduct, he will give us the maximum that it is possible to give, having in mind the offense which we have committed.

As Isaiah wrote, if we will return unto the Lord, "he will abundantly pardon."

—President J. Reuben Clark, Jr.

Quoted in James E. Faust, "The Atonement: Our Greatest Hope," *Ensign*, November 2001.

APPENDIX

It is impossible for us here in mortality to come to that state of perfection of which the Master spoke, but in this life we lay the foundation on which we will build in eternity.

—Harold B. Lee

Decisions for Successful Living (Salt Lake City: Deseret Book, 1973), 41.

Please don't nag yourself with thoughts of failure. Do not set goals far beyond your capacity to achieve. Simply do what you can do, in the best way you know, and the Lord will accept of your effort.

—Gordon B. Hinckley

"Rise to the Stature of the Divine within You," *Ensign*, November 1989, 94.

It is good to remember that being too hard on yourself when you make a mistake can be as negative as being too casual when real repentance is needed.

—Cecil O. Samuelson, Jr.

"Testimony," *Ensign*, May 2011, 41.

We are not perfect. The people around us are not perfect. People do things that annoy, disappoint, and anger. In this mortal life it will always be that way. . . . Part of the purpose of mortality is to learn how to let go of such things.

—Dieter F. Uchtdorf

"The Merciful Obtain Mercy," *Ensign*, May 2012, 77.

Becoming Christlike is a lifetime pursuit and very often involves growth and change that is slow, almost imperceptible. . . . The Lord is pleased with every effort, even the tiny, daily ones in which we strive to be more like Him. Though we may see that we have far to go on the road to perfection, we must not give up hope.

— Ezra Taft Benson

"A Mighty Change of Heart," *Ensign*, October 1989.

APPENDIX

My dear brothers and sisters, don't get discouraged if you stumble at times. Don't feel downcast or despair if you don't feel worth to be a disciple of Christ at all times. The first step to walking in righteousness is simply to try. We must try to believe. Try to learn of God: read the scriptures; study the words of His latter-day prophets; choose to listen to the Father, and do the things He asks of us. Try and keep on trying until that which seems difficult becomes possible—and that which seems only possible becomes habit and a real part of you.

—Dieter F. Uchtdorf

"The Love of God," *Ensign*, November 2009, 23.

INDEX

V

vulnerability 11, 12, 18, 54–56, 87, 103, 128

W

Walden Pond 129
web. *See* Internet
Welch, John W. 104
Whitney, Helen 119
Wilson, Larry Y. 83
Wirthlin, Joseph B. 152

Y

Young, Brigham 104

About the Author

Photo by Heather Clark

$\mathcal{S}$ue Bergin is a writer and hospice chaplain who lives in Orem, Utah. She drives throughout a five-county area to accompany dying men and women on their final journeys. She earned a bachelor's degree from Brigham Young University, a master's degree in journalism from Northwestern University, and a master of fine arts from UCLA in screenwriting. She is a board-certified clinical chaplain through The College of Pastoral Supervision and Psychotherapy.

Sue writes the Family Focus section for BYU Magazine and has written for many other publications, including the *Ensign*, the *San Francisco Chronicle*, *The Wall Street Journal*, and *Psychology Today*. She has been a public relations executive for BYU and has taught writing courses at BYU and the University of Utah.

ABOUT THE AUTHOR

Her dearest loves include time with family, small dinner parties with friends, rescuing animals, collecting art, and creating things with her hands—from soulful collages to crocheted earrings. She believes with all her heart that there really were gold plates, that the Book of Mormon is the most remarkable book ever written, and that Jesus Christ is our only hope, personally and globally.